Michel de Montaigne

IN DEFENSE
OF RAYMOND SEBOND

Translated, with an introduction, by
ARThUR H. BEATTIE
University of Arizona

UNGAR • NEW YORK

MILESTONES
OF THOUGHT
in the History of Ideas

General Editors
F. W. STROTHMANN
FREDERICK W. LOCKE
Stanford University
Eleventh Printing, 1987

Copyright © 1959 by
Frederick Ungar Publishing Co.

Printed in the United States of America

Library of Congress Catalog Card Number 59-15521

ISBN 0-8044-6519-3

INTRODUCTION

NEAR the beginning of his "In Defense of Raymond Sebond," Montaigne comments on the difficulty of translating an author whose style has distinctions of grace and beauty. He would be the first to deny that his own style has such qualities of art, yet it, too, is a difficult style to render into another language, at a distance of more than three and a half centuries. It is the most warmly personal style of any author of his day. It is learned and pedantic in its richness of allusions; it is discouragingly prolix in many passages in which detail is added to detail as in the conversation of a man of rich and varied experience, and of amazingly broad reading, who has the leisure to develop his ideas before a few sympathetic friends; it is sometimes quite familiar, since the author is chatting informally with us. "The style I like," declared Montaigne, "is a simple and natural style, the same on paper as in the mouth; a succulent and vigorous style . . . far removed from all affectation; disordered, loosely constructed, and bold . . .; not smacking of the schoolroom, cloister, or courtroom."

Montaigne is a gentleman of the Renaissance. In the main, the artist of the Middle Ages remains an anonymous craftsman; Montaigne, on the contrary, speaks much of himself, for it is his aim to know humanity as fully as possible, and what representative of the human race can he hope to know better than himself? He is a pioneer in probing into the subconscious wellsprings of emotions, attitudes, and behavior. What centuries later Walt Whitman was to declare about himself and his work, Montaigne could almost have affirmed too:

> I celebrate myself, and sing myself,
> And what I assume you shall assume,
> For every atom belonging to me as good belongs to you.

Montaigne is the inventor of that most personal of modern prose genres, the essay, and the word, in its literary sense, is his coinage. It suggests a tentative, groping effort to formulate ideas which, precisely because they grow out of one man's intimate experience, have a broad, universal value. Before Montaigne, the term had been used only in its literal sense of an attempt, or of an examiantion, an analysis (for *essay* and *assay* are variant forms of the same word).

Since, then, the essay is so clearly a reflection of the personality and experience of its author, we should, before discussing further the work of Michel de Montaigne, see something of his life. He was born in 1533 in his father's chateau of Montaigne in southwestern France near Bordeaux. His father, Pierre Eyquem, descended from a prosperous family of merchants, was a distinguished magistrate, was soon to serve as vice-mayor of Bordeaux, and, when his son Michel was entering young manhood, was to become mayor of that city. He had inherited the estates of Montaigne and was rebuilding and fortifying the old château. He had served in the military campaigns of the French in Italy and now led the life of a gentleman on his domains. Montaigne's mother was of a wealthy family of Portuguese or Spanish Jews who had been forced to emigrate and who had become Christians. Michel was one of eight children. Some of his brothers and sisters were to be converted to Protestantism, with the result that the religious disputes which divided France in the sixteenth century, and led to bitter civil conflict, had their repercussions within the author's own family.

Michel de Montaigne (for he adopted the name of the family's estate in lieu of the less high-sounding name of Eyquem which still, perhaps, bore a faint odor of the dried fish in which his grandfather had dealt) had a thoroughly Renaissance upbringing which he has described in an essay on education. His father had brought back from Italy extremely "progressive" ideas on the rearing of children. Eager that Michel should be a brilliant Latinist, he had a German tutor care for the child from infancy. Michel learned Latin as a mother tongue, hearing scarcely a word of French, or of Gascon dialect, until he had a complete and fluent mastery of the language of Cicero and Virgil. He then learned, through the direct experience of daily living, the speech of his native province. Montaigne is one of the earliest, and one of the most ardent, defenders of the "direct method" of language instruction.

As a consequence of this early initiation into the Latin language and Latin letters, Montaigne made extremely rapid progress in school and read much more widely among Roman writers than did other schoolboys in that age of rigorous training in the classics. He had no comparable facility in Greek, but Latin was to be for him as much a native tongue as French. His whole thinking is, of course, colored by the influence of the poets, historians, and philosophers of antiquity whom he had admired. In his "In Defense of Raymond Sebond," as in other essays, he sometimes misquotes his Latin sources, sometimes combines into a single passage lines which are not consecutive in the text, and thus proves his close familiarity with the works from which they are drawn, for he is on these occasions quoting from memory without referring to the books on his library shelves.

At the age of twenty-four, Montaigne began his career as a magistrate in the courts of Bordeaux. He continued this career until the age of thirty-eight, when he retired to the château of Montaigne, of which he had become the proprietor upon his father's death three years before. There are undoubtedly several reasons for this early retirement from the judiciary. One obvious explanation is that he found advancement barred because in the higher positions of the Bordeaux courts there were already several representatives of his family or of that of his wife. It is true, also, that he took seriously the problems of administration of his estates. He had perhaps political ambitions which led him to seek a broader sphere for his activities than a provincial lawcourt. In any event, he was on occasion to serve as counselor to both Henry III and Henry IV, and undertook quite delicate missions on the king's behalf. A careful reading of his "In Defense of Raymond Sebond" will reveal that he recognized the impossibility of achieving a purely impartial justice; no lawsuit is ever strictly a black and white affair, with all the wrong on one side and all the right on the other. Montaigne undoubtedly was distressed by the fact that every legal decision involves doubt and torment for the conscientious jurist.

In a tower of his château, Montaigne had assembled a distinguished library of over a thousand books. This remarkable private collection contained most of the significant works of classical antiquity, and many of the major modern works published during the past century since the invention of the printing press. Freed from his judicial duties, Montaigne found leisure to withdraw for long periods into the quiet of his library. Following a practice common among gentleman scholars of the day, as he read he copied passages he wished to remember, and made notes on the ideas his readings aroused in him. The essays have their origin in this custom. Traces of this purely bookish tradition will be found in the work on Raymond Sebond which contains developments borrowed from Sextus Empiricus and from Plutarch, and many passages quoted from Lucretius, Cicero, Virgil, and others.

The earliest form of his first essays is written during a time of violent civil conflict in 1572-74. At this period, Montaigne seeks intellectually to hold himself aloof from the torments of his country, and to achieve a Stoic calm. That his Stoicism grows out of a sincere admiration for Seneca and Cicero is certain; it is not, however, entirely in keeping with the fundamental nature of his own temperament, and the moment during which the Stoic attitude dominates in his thought is a brief one.

By 1576, the major influence over his thought and his writing is the interpretation of the skepticism of Pyrrho given by Sextus Empiricus. He will later, in successive editions, return to the early essays and add many touches of a more personal nature to adapt them to his purpose of studying mankind through an analysis of his own experience, and of his own thoughts and emotions. Already, however, by this date, when he begins "In Defense of Raymond Sebond," he has left behind the impersonal attitude of his earliest writings and is evolving toward his ultimate conception of the tone and purpose of the essays.

Montaigne's skepticism is never a nihilism. While he questions the ability of the human reason to arrive at an ultimate and incontrovertible truth, and while he therefore seeks to suspend his judgment, he nonetheless resolves to accept the doctrines of the Church in which he had been reared. He is doubtless sincere in his affirmation that only revelation can furnish us the truth, since reason cannot. At the same time, the experience of the civil wars has taught him that an effort to establish new doctrines and new modes of worship leads to bitter struggle and cruel bloodshed. Why subject oneself and one's fellows to these horrors, when reason can no more demonstrate the truth of the new doctrines than of the old? His hatred of violence inclines Montaigne toward the acceptance of traditional institutions and customs.

In 1580 Montaigne publishes the first two books of his *Essays*. One notes in these essays the transition from the early Stoicism to the skepticism of "In Defense of Raymond Sebond," and then a newer accent in the passages most recently written in which his enthusiasm for exploring the inner recesses of human nature begins to find expression. The death of his father, and even more the early death of the one close companion of his life with whom he had been able to share his thoughts and his feelings—his colleague in the courts of Bordeaux, Etienne de la Boétie—had helped make of Montaigne a Stoic. But his warm nature found that Stoic calm was unnatural in the midst of violent conflicts and widespread suffering, and thus the brief crisis of skepticism followed. He was brought out of that crisis by the normal evolution of his thought, and by the realization that he could enjoy life, in spite of the excruciating pain of kidney stones from which he now suffered periodically.

The 1580 edition of the *Essays* was well received. Immediately after its publication, Montaigne set out on a lengthy journey through Germany, Switzerland, and Italy, visiting many spas in the hope that the waters might relieve his painful malady. His universal curiosity is admirably revealed in his *Travel Journal.* People and manners interested him intensely. On a day when his pain was particularly severe, his eagerness would prompt him to spend long hours in the saddle in order to visit some historic site, or to pay a call on a fellow scholar.

During his absence, Montaigne was elected mayor of Bordeaux. Indeed, he had to cut short his visit in Italy and hurry home in 1581 to assume his official functions. The fact that two years later he was elected for a second term indicates that he had fulfilled his duties to the satisfaction of the electors.

The burdens of public office interrupted Montaigne's writing, but he returned to it to revise the earlier essays, and to compose the new ones which are, for the reader of today, among the most warmly human. A fifth edition of the *Essays* in 1588, in which the third book appears for the first time, was the last published in Montaigne's lifetime. He was not to abandon his literary offspring, however, and in the margins of the edition of 1588 he wrote many modifications and added many new passages which were included in an edition of 1595.

This edition was prepared and published by his executors, for in 1592, quietly, during the performance of a mass in his room at Montaigne, death brought to an end the pains which had long racked his body, but which had never conquered his spirit.

"In Defense of Raymond Sebond" is much the longest of Montaigne's essays. In the present edition it has been shortened considerably by the omission of numerous exam-

ples of the intelligence of animals, and of various other
lengthy developments. All such omissions are indicated by a
series of points [. . .].

The essay itself explains Montaigne's interest in the
work of natural theology written in the fifteenth century by
the Spanish physician, Raymond Sebond. Montaigne, at his
father's request, had earlier translated it from Latin into
French. His defense of Sebond's demonstration of the existence of God and the truth of the doctrines of the Christian
faith by conclusions drawn from observation of the phenom-
ena of nature is addressed to a princess who may be identified
as Marguerite de Valois, daughter of King Henry II, and
wife of Henry of Navarre, the future Henry IV of France.
It has been pointed out that Montaigne supports Sebond
somewhat as the rope supports the hanged man, for his skepticism regarding the powers of the human reason seems
equally effectively to destroy the value of Sebond's arguments and those of his critics.

Much of the essay seems, indeed, to have little to do
with Sebond. Perhaps the bulk of it had been written earlier
as an attack on the excessive claims of dogmatic philosophy,
and then adapted to serve as part of the answer to the critics
of Sebond. For us, its major importance lies in the fact that
it is the fullest and most effective presentation of Montaigne's skepticism.

It serves, too, as a sort of compendium of Renaissance
knowledge of the philosophical and literary texts of Greek
and, especially, of Roman antiquity. Quotations from and
allusions to Latin authors are abundant. Many of these quotations are from poets. For his Renaissance readers, Montaigne could properly leave in the original tongue all the
passages he quoted; in the present translation, they have
been put into a metrical English which has no claim to literary excellence, but which at least follows closely the original text.

No other essay of Montaigne has had so marked an
influence on successive generations of philosophers and lit-

erary artists. The notions of the relativity of truth and of justice, of the insignificance of man in nature, of the effect of external circumstances and of emotions and states of mind upon our judgments, and of man's close relationship to the lower animals, have been especially stimulating. Echoes of Montaigne's treatment of them will be found in the work of many writers of every period from Montaigne's day to our own. The reader who is already familiar with Pascal will find in this essay the source of a number of the central developments in the *Pensées* dealing with justice, with the limitations of man's reason, with the slight influences which upset his equilibrium, and with his puny and wretched condition.

"In Defense of Raymond Sebond" is the masterpiece of Montaigne's critical period of skepticism—a skepticism which questions the validity of the conventional teachings of philosophy, and of the vaunted truths of science, so quickly outmoded and replaced, but which leaves the door open for the acquisition of a surer knowledge of self and of man when the prejudices of traditional learning have been set aside. It has a still broader value as a document of primary importance in the whole history of skeptical thought, and as a major source of an essentially modern current of ideas—the notion of the relative nature of customs and of morals, of justice and of truth.

A.H.B.

SELECTED BIBLIOGRAPHY

In French

Several fine scholarly editions of the *Essais* have appeared in this century. Especially noteworthy are those of Pierre Villey, 3 vols., Alcan, Paris, 1930-31, and of Jean Plattard, 6 vols., Fernand Roches, Paris, 1931-33.

The most compact and most convenient edition for the general reader is that in one volume by Albert Thibaudet for the "Bibliothèque de la Pléiade," NRF, Paris, 1950.

In English

The classic English translation is that of John Florio, of 1603. It is readily available today in the Everyman's Library, 3 vols., E. P. Dutton and Co., New York.

Two recent translations are recommended. These are.

(1) Michel de Montaigne, *Essays,* translated by Jacob Zeitlin, 3 vols., Knopf, New York, 1934-36. Excellent introduction and commentaries.

(2) *The Complete Works of Montaigne* (Essays, Travel Journal, Letters), 1 vol., translated by Donald M. Frame, Stanford University Press, 1957. A fine translation of the *Essays,* and the only convenient English version of the other works.

Selections from the *Essays,* with an introduction by André Gide, are available in the volume *Montaigne,* of "The Living Thoughts Library," David McKay, New York, 1939.

SOURCES OF MONTAIGNE'S
LATIN QUOTATIONS

It would be idle to attempt to indicate the source of all the ideas and developments which Montaigne borrows from Latin writings. The source of the major direct quotations is, however, given in brackets following the passage cited. Works best known by an English title are so listed in the references, while for less familiar works the Latin title is given. The authors and works to which reference is made are listed below.

If but one title by an author appears in this list, only the author's name is given in the references. Thus the reference [Lucretius III, 613] means that the quotation is drawn from Book III of *De rerum natura,* beginning with line 613. In some instances, three numbers will appear, thus: [Horace, *Epistles* I, v, 6]. This quotation begins at line 6 of the fifth epistle in the first book. Prose quotations will be identified by book (in Roman numerals) and chapter (in Arabic numerals).

Saint Augustine: *De civitate Dei*
                 De ordine
Catullus: *Carmina*
Cicero: *Academica*
       De divinatione
       De fato
       De finibus
       De natura deorum
       Tusculanae disputationes
Horace: *Epistulae*
       Carmina
Juvenal: *Saturae*
Livy: *Ab urbe condita*
Lucretius: *De rerum natura*
Manilius: *Astronomica*

Ovid: *Metamorphoses*
    Remedia amoris
    Tristia
Pliny: *Historia naturalis*
Quintilian: *Institutiones oratoriae*
Sallust: *Bellum Jugurthinum*
Seneca, L. Annaeus: *Epistulae morales*
    De ira
    Oedipus
    Quaestiones naturales
Seneca, M. Annaeus: *Suasoriae*
Tacitus: *De Germania*
Vegetius: *De re militari*
Virgil: *Aeneis*
    Georgica

CONTENTS

CHAPTER I

God and Creation

[*Summary*—In the opening section of the essay, here given in its entirety, Montaigne explains how Raymond Sebond's work on the truths of the Christian religion, as proved by the marvels of creation and the nature of man, came into his father's hands. Montaigne notes that some Christians believe it impious to utilize appeals to reason to bolster belief in truths which must be accepted on faith. In the course of his argument that man's rational faculties may properly be used in support of religious faith, Montaigne assails the shallowness of the belief of Christians of his day. He points out the opportunistic nature of the teachings of both Catholic and Protestant parties in the bitter civil wars being fought in France, and deplores the absence of true Christianity which would be revealed through the gentle, noble, and virtuous lives of those who profess it. The denial of divine control of the universe is an unnatural attitude, and the atheist himself, faced with the imminence of death, tends to turn to superstition. Creation bears the marks of God's greatness. Sebond's arguments based on the revelation of God's nature and his power are more forceful than any his opponents have been able to muster.]

Sebond's book and Montaigne's
translation of it.

Knowledge is, in truth, a very useful and important accomplishment. Those who disdain it reveal clearly enough their stupidity; but I do not, however, set its worth at the extremely high value which some attribute to it, like Herillus the philosopher who believed that in it resided the sovereign good, and who considered that knowledge could make us wise and happy. I believe neither this, nor what others have said—that learning is the mother of all virtue, and that all

1

vice is the product of ignorance. If that is true, it is subject to a long interpretation.

My home has long been open to scholarly men and is well known to them, for my father, who presided over it for fifty years and more, fired by that new zeal with which King Francis I embraced letters and gave them prestige, sought with great care and expense the acquaintance of learned men, receiving them in his home as holy persons whom God had selected to inspire with wisdom, noting their maxims and their sayings as oracles, and this with a reverence and devotion all the greater because he had little authority to judge them, for he had no acquaintance with letters any more than his predecessors had. As for myself, I am fond of them, but I do not worship them.

Among such visitors was Pierre Bunel, a man of great reputation for learning in his time. Having stayed a few days at Montaigne as my father's guest, with other men of his sort, he presented him, on leaving, a book entitled *Natural Theology, or the Book of Creatures,* by Master Raymond Sebond. And because the Italian and Spanish languages were familiar to my father, and because this book is written in a sort of jargon of Spanish with Latin endings, he hoped that with very little help my father might find it of value, and he recommended it to him as a very useful book, especially fitting for the particular time at which he gave it to him. It was the moment when the new ideas of Luther were beginning to gain a following and to shake in many places our long-established belief. In his fear of the consequences of Lutheranism, Pierre Bunel was most clear-sighted, foreseeing well, by logical deduction, that this beginning of illness would readily decline into an execrable atheism; for the masses, not having the faculty of judging things in themselves, and swayed by chance and mere appearances, once they have been allowed the boldness to disdain and to examine opinions which they had earlier held in extreme reverence such as those which pertain to salvation, and once certain tenets of their religion have been weighed and put in doubt,

immediately afterwards are prone to cast into a similar uncertainty all the other elements of their belief which had had
for them no more authority or no better foundation than
those which had been overthrown. They then shake off, like
a tyrannical yoke, all the impressions which they had received through the authority of laws or respect for established custom,

> For eagerly one tramples underfoot
> What he had too much dreaded previously,
> [Lucretius V, 1139]

undertaking henceforth to accept nothing to which they have
not given, after examination, a special consent.

Now a few days before his death my father, having by
chance come across this book under a pile of other abandoned
papers, instructed me to put it into French for him. It is
good to translate authors like this one, where there is little
but the matter to present; but those who have been much
concerned with the grace and elegance of their language
are dangerous to undertake, especially when one seeks to
translate them into a weaker idiom. That was a quite strange
and new occupation for me; but being by chance at leisure
at that moment, and not being able to refuse anything re-
quested by the best father who ever was, I accomplished
the task as best I could. This gave my father a special pleasure, and he left instructions that it be printed. This request
was carried out after his death.

I admired this author's imagination for the beauties it
created, the structure of his work for its logic and order, and
his purpose for its piety. Because many people find pleasure
in reading it, and especially ladies to whom we must seek
more particularly to be helpful, I have often found myself
in a position to assist them in freeing their book from two
principal objections which are made against it. Its purpose is
bold and courageous, for it undertakes by human and natural
arguments to bolster and defend against atheists all the
articles of the Christian religion. In accomplishing this end,

I find it so firm and so successful that I do not believe it is possible to do better in that argument, and I am of the opinion that none has equalled it. This work seeming to me too rich and beautiful for an author whose name is so unfamiliar, and concerning whom all we know is that he was a Spaniard practicing medicine in Toulouse about two hundred years ago, I once inquired of Adrianus Turnebus,[1] who knew everything, what this book might be; he gave it as his opinion that it was drawn from St. Thomas Aquinas and represented the quintessence of a writing of his, for really, he said, the mind of St. Thomas, full of an infinite erudition and admirable subtlety, was alone capable of such inventions. All in all, whoever the author may be (and there is no reason for taking from Sebond that honor without further evidence) he was a very capable man gifted with many fine talents.

Reason may bolster religious truths accepted by faith.

The first criticism that is made of his work is that Christians are wrong to seek to base on human reasoning their belief which is conceived only through faith and by a special inspiration of divine grace. In this objection it seems that there is some zeal of piety, and for this reason we must with all the more gentleness and respect try to satisfy those who propose it. The task would better become a man versed in theology than me who am ignorant of it.

However, it is my opinion that in a matter so divine and lofty, so far exceeding human intelligence as is this truth concerning which it has pleased God to enlighten us, it is indeed necessary that he lend us still his aid, by an extraordinary and privileged favor, so that we may be able to conceive that truth and accept it within us. I do not believe that purely human means are at all capable of this;

---

[1] French scholar, and translator of many Greek texts. (1512-1565)

and if they were, so many rare and excellent souls, and so abundantly endowed with natural gifts, would not have failed in the centuries of antiquity to attain that knowledge. It is faith alone which embraces wholeheartedly and surely the high mysteries of our religion. But that does not mean that it is not a very fine and praiseworthy enterprise to utilize also in the service of our faith the natural and human instruments which God has given to us. One must not doubt that it is the most honorable use that we can make of them, and there is no undertaking or purpose more worthy of a Christian man than to aim by all his studies and thoughts to embellish, extend, and magnify the truth of his belief. We are not limited to serving God in spirit and soul; we owe him also, and we render to him, a bodily reverence; we employ our very limbs, and our movements, and external objects in honoring him. Similarly we must accompany our faith with all the reason that is in us, but always with this reservation that we do not consider that our faith depends upon our reason, nor that our efforts and reasonings can reach a supernatural and divine knowledge.

If that faith does not enter our being by an extraordinary infusion, if it enters it not merely by reasoning, but even by any human means, it is not there in its dignity and its splendor. And certainly I fear, however, that we possess faith only through such channels. If we were linked to God through the bond of a living faith, if we were linked to God in his way, not in our own, if we had a divine footing and foundation, human events would not have the power to upset us as they do; our citadel would not be inclined to surrender to such a weak battery; the love of new things, the authority of princes, the good fortune of a faction, the rash and fortuitous change of our opinions, would not have the power to shake and alter our belief; we should not let it be disturbed by some new argument, not even by the persuasion of all the rhetoric which ever was; we should endure those waves with an inflexible and unmoved firmness,

> As a vast cliff hurls back the battering waves,
> And scatters roaring waters round about,
> With its opposing bulk.
> [Imitated from Virgil, *Aeneid* VII, 587]

*The Christian's life should
conform to his beliefs.*

If this ray of the divine touched us at all, it would be
evident in everything; not only our words but also our deeds
would bear its glow and luster. Everything that came from
us would be seen illuminated with that noble light. We
ought to be ashamed that among the sects of men there was
never any member, whatever difficulty and strangeness his
doctrine might involve, who failed completely to make his
behavior and his life conform to it; and yet such a divine and
celestial teaching as ours marks Christians only by what they
say.

Do you wish an illustration of this? Compare our
manner of living with that of a Mohammedan, of a pagan.
We always remain inferior, in the very respect where the
superiority of our religion ought to make us shine in excellence at an extreme and incomparable distance; and one
ought to be able to say: "Are they so just, so charitable, so
kind? They are, then, Christians." All other aspects are
common to all religions: hope, confidence, events, ceremonies, penitence, martyrs. The peculiar mark of our truth
ought to be our virtue, as it is also the most celestial and
most difficult mark, and as it is the most worthy product of
truth. Yet our good Saint Louis was right when that Tartar
king who had become a Christian announced his intention
of coming to Lyons to kiss the feet of the pope and to recognize there the saintliness which he hoped to find in our
manner of living. Saint Louis urgently dissuaded him, lest
on the contrary our licentious mode of life might make him
lose his taste for such a holy belief. Although it turned out
in quite the opposite way later for that other who, having
gone to Rome for the same purpose, seeing there the disso-

lute life of the prelates and people of that time, accepted all the more firmly our religion, considering how much strength and divinity it must have to maintain its dignity and splendor among so much corruption and in such vicious hands.

If we had a single drop of faith, we should move the mountains from their place, says holy scripture; our actions, which would be guided and and accompanied by divinity, would not be merely human; there would be something miraculous about them as about our belief. "Quickly you learn the lesson of a virtuous and blessed life if you believe." [Quintilian XII 11]

Some persuade their society that they believe what they do not believe. Others, in greater number, persuade themselves of it, unable to comprehend what believing really is.

Religion is made to serve
worldly, political ends.

And we think it strange if, in the wars which afflict our state at the present time, we see events vacillate and take various forms, in a common and ordinary way. It is because we bring to them nothing but our own. The justice which is in one of the parties is there only as an ornament and disguise; it is indeed invoked, but it is neither received, nor harbored, nor espoused. It is there as in the mouth of the lawyer, not as in the heart and affection of one deeply involved. God extends properly his extraordinary help to faith and to religion, not to our passions. Men are the leaders in our conflicts, and they make of religion an instrument to serve their ends; it ought to be quite the contrary.

Consider if it is not by our hands that we shape religion, drawing as from wax so many contrary figures from a rule so straight and so firm. When has that been more evident than in France nowadays? Those who have seized it on the left hand, those who have seized it on the right, those who use black to portray it and those who use white, employ religion in such a similar way in their violent and ambitious enterprises, behave according to a pattern so identical in excess and injustice, that they render doubtful and hard to believe the contradictory opinions which they claim to hold concerning the thing on which depend the conduct and principle of our life. Can one see come out of the same school and the same doctrine ways of acting more uniform, more completely identical?

See the horrible impudence with which we toss back and forth arguments concerning God's will, and how irreligiously we have both rejected them and re-adopted them as fortune has changed sides in these public storms. This most solemn proposition: "Whether it is permissible for the subject to rebel and take up arms against his prince for the defense of religion," remember in what mouths this past year the affirmative was the buttress of one party, the negative the buttress of what other party?[2] And now hear from what quarter come the proclamation and teaching of both these doctrines, and consider whether arms are any less noisy in support of one cause than of the other. And we burn people who say that one must subject truth to the yoke of our expediency. And how much worse is France in doing it rather than merely saying it?

Let us confess the truth: were one to sift out of the army, even the average legitimate army, those who participate in it solely through the zeal of a religious devotion, and also those who are concerned only with the protection of the laws of their country or the service of the prince, one would not be able to form with them a complete company of soldiers. Whence comes it that there are so few who have maintained a uniform will and effort in our public disturbances and that we see them sometimes advance at a walk, sometimes gallop at top speed, and the same men sometimes harm our cause by their violence and harshness, sometimes

---

[2] The Protestant faction maintained the right to take up arms against the King in defense of religion until the death of Henry III in 1589; with Henry of Navarre now the legitimate heir to the throne, the Roman Catholic party used the same argument after that date. One readily sees at about what date Montaigne added this statement to his essay.

by their lack of zeal, their softness, and their slowness, unless it be that they are moved by personal and casual considerations according to the varying nature of which they bestir themselves?

This I see clearly, that we readily give to religion only the services which flatter our passions. There is no hostility so fine as Christian hostility. Our zeal does marvels when it supports our inclination toward hatred, cruelty, ambition, avarice, slander, rebellion. On the contrary, toward kindness, gentleness, temperance, unless by a miracle some rare quirk of character drives it in that direction, it neither runs nor flies.

Our religion is made to root out vices; we use it to cover them, feed them, encourage them.

One must not offer God straw instead of grain (as the popular saying goes). If we believed in him, I do not say through faith, but with a simple belief, indeed (and I say it to our great confusion) if we believed in him and knew him as we might some other matter, as we might know one of our companions, we should love him above all other things for the infinite goodness and beauty which shine in him; at least he would occupy in our affection the same rank as wealth, pleasures, glory, and our friends.

The best of us does not fear to offend him as he fears offending his neighbor, his relative, his master. Is there a mind so simple that, having on the one side the object of one of our vicious pleasures, and on the other, equally clearly known and understood, the state of an immortal glory, it would give the latter in exchange for the former? And yet we often renounce that glory out of pure disdain: for what desire attracts us to blasphemy unless by chance the very desire to offend?

Convictions are weak if external
events alter them.

The philosopher Antisthenes, as he was being initiated into the Orphic mysteries, was told by the priest that those who devoted themselves to that religion were destined to receive after their death eternal and perfect gifts. "Why, then, don't you die yourself?" he asked the priest. Diogenes, more abruptly according to his manner, and on a somewhat different subject, said to the priest who was exhorting him similarly to join his order so that he might attain the blessings of the next world: "Don't you want me to believe that Agesilaus and Epaminondas, such great men, will be wretched, and that you, who are only a fool, will be blessed because you are a priest?"

If we received with the same authority as a philosophical discourse these great promises of eternal blessedness, we should no longer view death with the horror in which we now hold it.

> No longer would the dying man lament
> His dissolution, but he would rejoice
> To leave the body as the snake is freed
> Of its worn skin, or as the stag grown old
> Lets fall at last its horns now overlong.
> [Lucretius III, 613]

I wish to be dissolved, we should say, and to be with Jesus Christ. The force of Plato's teaching concerning the immortality of the soul encouraged indeed some of his disciples to seek death in order to enjoy more promptly the hopes which he gave them.

All that is a very obvious sign that we receive our religion only in our way, and by our hands, and not otherwise than other religions are received. We happened to be in the region where it was observed; or we esteem its antiquity or the authority of the men who have taught it; or we fear the threats which it directs against unbelievers; or we are drawn by its promises. Those considerations must be employed for our belief, but as secondary supports: they are based on human ties. A different region, other witnesses, similar promises and threats, might impress upon us in the same way a contrary belief. We are Christians for the same reason that we are either Perigordians or Germans.

As for what Plato says, that there are few men so firm in atheism that a pressing danger does not bring them back to the recognition of divine power, such an influence does not touch a true Christian. It is only for mortal and human religions to be received or rejected according to the situation in which we find ourselves. What faith must that be which cowardice and weakness of heart implant and nourish within us? A strange faith which believes what it believes only because it does not have the courage not to believe it! Can a vicious passion such as weakness and terror produce within our soul anything which is well ordered?

Atheists establish, says Plato, by the authority of their judgment, that what is related about hell and future torments is false. But, since the opportunity to test it presents itself when old age or illnesses bring them close to their death, the terror which these inspire fills them then with a new belief through the horror of the condition which is approaching for them. And, because such impressions make hearts fearful, he forbids in his laws any teachings about these menaces, and the belief that from the gods there can come to man any harm unless for his greater good, when the case does present itself, and for a salutary effect. They tell of Bion that, corrupted by the atheistic teachings of Theodorus, he had long been wont to make sport of religious men; but when death came suddenly upon him he gave himself over to the most extreme superstitions, as if the gods absented themselves and came back according to Bion's situation.

Plato and these examples tend to conclude that we are brought back to belief in God either by love or by force. Atheism being, so to speak, a doctrine unnatural and monstrous, difficult also and troublesome to establish in the human mind, however insolent and disordered that mind may be, one has seen a rather large number of persons, out of vanity and out of pride in imagining uncommon opinions which aim at reforming the world, affect the profession of atheism as a pose; these persons, if they are foolish enough, are not strong enough, however, to have established it firmly in their conscience. They will not fail to raise clasped hands toward heaven if you give them a good sword-thrust in the chest. And, when fear or illness will have got the better of that licentious fervor of fickle mood, they will not fail to turn about quite discreetly and conform to public beliefs and practices. A seriously digested dogma is one thing; these superficial impressions which, born of the idleness of an unbalanced mind, go swimming rashly and uncertainly in fantasy are another. Men so wretched and scatterbrained, who try to be worse than they can!

The error of paganism, and the ignorance of our holy truth, permitted that great soul of Plato (but great with merely a human greatness) to fall also into this other related mistake, namely that children and old men are more susceptible to religion, as if it were born of and drew its prestige from our weakness.

God revealed in creation
as Sebond shows.

The tie which ought to link our judgment and our will, which ought to entwine our soul and join it to our creator, that tie ought to derive its windings and its strength, not from our ponderings, our reasonings, and our passions, but from a divine and supernatural embrace, having only one form, countenance, and luster, which is the authority of God and his grace. Now, our heart and our soul being governed and commanded by faith, it is reasonable that the soul should draw to the service of its goal all the other parts of our being according to their potentialities. Thus it is not believable that all this creation should bear no marks imprinted by the hand of that great architect, and that there should be no image in the things of this world reflecting in some way the worker who built and formed them. God has left on these lofty works the stamp of his divinity, and it is purely the fault of our imbecility that we cannot discover it. That is what he tells us himself: that he makes manifest to us his invisible operations through the visible ones. Sebond gave himself over to this worthy study, and he shows us how there is no fragment of creation which belies its creator. It would be an insult to divine goodness if the universe did not consent to our belief. The sky, the earth, the elements, our body, and our soul, all things work together toward that end; one has only to find the way to use them. They instruct us, if we are capable of hearing. For this world is a sacred temple, within which man is placed in order to contemplate sculptures which are not wrought by mortal hand but which divine thought has made perceptible: the sun, the stars, the waters, and the earth, with the purpose of representing to us the things which can be understood. The invisible things of God, says Saint Paul, become apparent through the creation of the world when we consider his eternal wisdom and his divinity through his works. [Cf. *Romans* I, 20]

> God hides not from the earth the sight of heaven;
> Its ceaseless revolutions overhead
> Unveil to us all aspects of its body;
> Himself he thus reveals and so impresses
> That we may know him well, and contemplate
> His motions and pay reverence to his laws.
> [Manilius IV, 907]

Now our human reasonings and discourses are like heavy and sterile matter; the grace of God is their form; it is that grace which gives them individuality and worth. Just as the virtuous actions of Socrates and Cato remain vain and useless for not having had their proper goal, for not having regard for the love and obedience due to the true creator of all things, and for not having known God, so it is with our ideas and our words. They have body, but it is a shapeless mass, without form and without light, unless faith and the grace of God are added to them. Faith coming to color and illumine the reasonings of Sebond, it makes them firm and solid; they are capable of serving as a companion and first guide to an apprentice to put him on the road toward this knowledge; they form him somewhat, and make him capable of the grace of God, through the efficacy of which our belief is afterwards completed and perfected. I know a man of authority, well versed in letters, who confessed to me that he had been led back out of error and misbelief through the arguments of Sebond. And even were one to strip them of that ornament and support and approbation of faith, and to take them for purely human inventions, devised to combat those who are cast into the dreadful and horrible darkness of irreligion, they will still remain as solid and firm as any others of the same order which one can bring up against them. We are thus in a position to say to our opponents:

> If you have something better, bring it forth,
> Or else surrender.
> [Horace, *Epistles* I, v, 6]

Let them recognize the strength of our proofs, or let them show us elsewhere, and on some other subject, ones better put together and better supported.

CHAPTER II

Man and the Lower Animals

[*Summary*—In an effort to attack the validity of the arguments used against Sebond by freethinking critics, sure of the capacity of their reason to deal with all subjects, Montaigne seeks to show that man's pride in his exalted position among the creatures of the universe is but a vain presumption. He presents man as a petty being lost in the infinity of creation. To demonstrate the falsity of human claims to superiority over other creatures, he compares at great length man to the lower animals. Montaigne rejects completely any notion that animals are mere automatons, unfeeling and unreasoning. With the aid of numerous anecdotes borrowed in the main from writers of antiquity, he presents the beasts as often excelling man in meeting, with the help of their reasoning powers, the problems and difficulties which confront them. Many of these examples are omitted in this edition. It is not, however, Montaigne's aim to prove that man is inferior to the other creatures which inhabit this world. He seeks, rather, to demonstrate that man, for all his proud claims, is one with the other animals, of a status neither more abject nor more exalted than theirs. Put thus in his proper place, man can no longer boast of a privileged rank nor exult in the powers of his reason as a unique gift which permits him to understand all things.]

*Man's reason is a
puny instrument.*

Without realizing it, I have already touched somewhat on the second objection against Sebond to which I had intended to reply.

Some say that his arguments are weak, and unfitted to verify what he sets out to prove, and they undertake to upset

15

them readily. One must strike at these critics a little more roughly, for they are more dangerous and more malicious than the first. One readily bends the meaning of the writings of others in the direction of the opinions which he has pre-formed within himself; and an atheist is confident that he can interpret all authors in an atheistic way, infecting inno-cent matter with his own venom. Such persons have certain prejudices which destroy their appreciation of Sebond's argu-ments. Moreover, it seems to them that they have been given a free rein by being set free to combat our religion with purely human weapons, our religion which they would not dare attack in its full majesty of authority and command. The approach I use to reduce this mad zeal, and which seems to me the most fitting, is to crush and trample under foot pride and human presumption; to make them feel the empti-ness, the vanity, and the nothingness of man; to snatch from their hands the puny weapons of their reason; to make them bow their heads and bite the dust before the authority and reverence of divine majesty. To it alone belong knowledge and wisdom; it alone can enjoy self-esteem, and from it we borrow whatever we value and prize in ourselves. "For the god allows none but himself to have lofty thoughts." [Her-odotus VII, 10]

Let us destroy this presumption, the first foundation of the tyranny of the evil spirit, "For God resisteth the proud, and giveth grace to the humble." [I *Peter* V, 5] Intelligence is in all the gods, says Plato, and in very few men.

Now it is nonetheless great consolation to the Christian to see our mortal and perishable instruments so properly matched with our holy and divine faith that when he uses them upon matters of a mortal and perishable nature also, they prove no more uniformly or effectively appropriate. Let us see, then, whether man has in his power other argu-ments stronger than Sebond's, or whether, indeed, he can arrive at any certitude by argument and reasoning.

For Saint Augustine, pleading against such people, has

occasion to reproach them with injustice in considering false those parts of our belief which our reason fails to establish; and in order to show that rather many things can be and have been whose nature and causes our reason cannot determine, he calls to their attention certain known and undeniable experiences concerning which man confesses that he understands nothing; and in this, as in all other things, he reveals his diligent and ingenious inquiry. One must go further, and teach them that it is unnecessary, to demonstrate the weakness of their reason, to go seeking unusual examples, but that reason is so deficient and so blind that there is nothing so clear and easy that it is sufficiently clear for it; that easy and difficult are one and the same to it; that all subjects equally, and nature in general, lie outside its jurisdiction and its grasp.

What does truth preach to us when it instructs us to flee worldly philosophy, when it inculcates in us so often that its wisdom is only folly in the sight of God; that, of all vanities, the most vain is man; that the man who is proud of his knowledge does not yet know what knowledge is; and that man, who is nothing, is deluding and deceiving himself if he thinks he is something? These maxims of the Holy Spirit express so clearly and so precisely what I wish to maintain that I should need no other proof against people who would bow with complete submission and obedience to its authority. But the people we are concerned with choose to be whipped to their own cost and will permit one to combat their reasoning only with reason itself.

Man's insignificance in nature.

Let us then consider for the moment man alone, without outside help, armed only with his own weapons, and stripped of grace and divine understanding, which are all his honor, his strength, and the foundation of his being. Let us see what kind of figure he cuts in such a fine array. Let him make me understand by the effort of his reason upon what foundations he has built those great advantages which he thinks he has over all other creatures. What has convinced him that this admirable motion of the vault of heaven, the eternal light of those torches revolving so proudly above his head, the awe-inspiring movements of that infinite sea, were established and have continued for so many centuries for his convenience and in order to serve him? Is it possible to imagine anything so ridiculous as that wretched and puny creature, who is not even master of himself, exposed to offenses from all things, and who yet proclaims himself master and emperor of the universe, concerning which it is not within his power to know the slightest part, let alone govern it? And this privilege that he attributes to himself of being alone in this great creation in having the capacity to recognize its beauty and understand its structure, in being able to give thanks to the architect and to note the balance of income and outlay of the world—who placed the seal upon this privilege accorded him? Let him show us the patent of this fine and great prerogative.

Was it granted in favor of the wise only? It concerns few people, then. Are the foolish and wicked worthy of such an extraordinary favor, and they who are the worst part of creation, should they be given a privileged position above all the rest?

Shall we believe on this score him who says: "For whom then shall we say that the world was made? Doubtless for animate beings who have the use of reason. These are gods and men, to whom surely nothing is superior." [Cicero, *De natura deorum* II, 53] It is impossible ever to ridicule sufficiently the impudence of thus associating gods and men.

But, puny creature that he is, what has man in himself worthy of such a privileged position? Considering the incorruptible life of the heavenly bodies, their beauty, their greatness, their movement continued according to so precise a rule:

When we lift up our eyes to the celestial vaults
Of this great universe, and toward the heaven set
With shining stars, and when we call to mind the course
Of moon and sun;

[Lucretius V, 1205]

considering, too, the domination and power which those
bodies have not only over our lives and the conditions of our
fortune,

For he has made the deeds and lives of men
Dependent on the stars,

[Manilius III, 58]

but over our very inclinations, our reasonings, our wills
which they govern, drive and stir at the mercy of their
influences, as our reason teaches us and reveals,

For reason recognizes that those stars we see
So distant from us, govern men by hidden laws;
That movements of the universe entire are ruled
By periodic causes, and the turns of fate
Revealed by certain signs;

[Manilius I, 60]

seeing that not a single man, not a king, escapes their influence, but that monarchies, empires, and this whole world
here below move in accord with the slightest tremor of the
celestial movements,

How great are the effects the slightest motion brings:
So mighty is that power which governs even kings!

[Manilius I, 55 and IV, 93]

if our virtue, our vices, our competence and learning, and
this very conclusion which we draw concerning the power
of the stars, and this comparison of them with ourselves, if
all that comes, as our reason judges, by their means and their
favor,

> One, mad with love,
> Is doomed to cross the sea and Troy town overthrow;
> Another's fated to draw up a nation's laws;
> Here children slay their parents, and parents slay their
>   sons;
> And armed against his brother, one fights in cruel affray.
> This war's not of our doing; fate wills these agitations,
> And makes them hurt themselves, slashing each other's
>   limbs.
> And fate wills too that I should thus discourse of fate;
>   [Manilius IV, 79 and 118]

if we owe to heaven's distribution this share of reason which we possess, how can it make us heaven's equal? How can its essence and its conditions be subject to our learning? Everything which we see in those bodies awes us. "What was the effort, what were the instruments, the levers, the machines, the workers who erected so vast an edifice?" [Cicero, *De natura deorum* I, 8] Why do we consider them without soul, and life, and reason? Have we recognized in them some heavy and unfeeling stupidity, we whose only relationship to them is one of obedience? Shall we say that we have seen in no other creature but man the employment of a reasoning soul? What then! Have we seen anything similar to the sun? Must we say that it does not exist because we have never seen anything like it? And that its movements do not exist because they are without parallel? If what we have not observed does not exist, our learning is wonderfully restricted: "How narrow are the limits of our mind!" [Cicero, *De natura deorum* I, 31] Is it not a dream of human vanity to make of the moon a celestial earth, to imagine on it mountains and valleys as Anaxagoras did, to set up there human habitations and abodes, and to establish there colonies for our convenience as Plato and Plutarch do, and of our earth to make a light-giving and luminous star? "Among other infirmities of human nature is this blindness of the mind which not only forces it to err, but which makes it love its errors. [Seneca, *De ira* II, 10] "The

corruptible body weighs down the soul, and its earthly cov-
ering oppresses it even in the exercise of thought." [St.
Augustine, *City of God* XII, 15, citing *Book of Wisdom*]

Man's superiority over animals
a delusion based on pride.

Presumption is our natural and original malady. The
most calamitous and fragile of all creatures is man, and at
the same time the proudest. He sees and feels himself placed
here in the mire and dung of the world, attached and fixed
in the worst, most lifeless, and most corrupt part of the universe, on the meanest floor of the house and the farthest
removed from the vault of heaven, with animals of the
worst condition of the three;[3] and he goes installing himself
in his imagination above the circle of the moon and bringing the heavens beneath his feet. It is by the vanity of this
same imagination that he makes himself God's equal, that
he ascribes to himself divine attributes, that he winnows
himself and separates himself from the mass of other creatures, determines the share allowed the animals, his col-
leagues and companions, and distributes to them such elements of faculties and powers as seem good to him. How
does he know, by the effort of his intelligence, what inwardly
and secretly moves animals? By what comparison of them
with ourselves does he deduce the stupidity which he attributes to them?

When I play with my cat, who knows whether she is
not making me her pastime more than I make her mine?
Plato, in depicting the golden age under Saturn, counts
among the principal advantages of the man of those days
the ability he had to communicate with the animals, for
questioning them and learning from them, he knew the real
qualities of each; in that way he acquired a quite perfect
understanding and wisdom, and in consequence conducted
his life far more happily than we can do. Do we need a

---

[3] Those that fly, that swim, and that live on the ground.

better proof to judge human presumption concerning animals? That great author gave it as his opinion that so far as the corporal form which nature gave them is concerned, she had regard, in the main, only for the prognostications which one was accustomed to draw from them in his day.

Speech not a power
peculiar to man.

This defect which prevents communication between them and ourselves, why isn't it as much ours as theirs? It's anybody's guess whose fault it is that we don't understand one another, for we do not understand them any more than they understand us. For this same reason, they may consider us stupid as we do them. It's no great marvel if we do not understand them (after all, we don't understand Basques or Troglodytes). However, some have boasted that they understood them, like Apollonius of Tyana, Melampus, Teiresias, Thales, and others. . . . We must note that the beasts and ourselves are in the same situation. We have some general understanding of their meaning, and so do they of ours, in about the same degree. They flatter us, threaten us, and coax us; and we do the same to them.

Moreover, we discover quite obviously that among themselves there is a full and complete communication and that they understand one another, not only within their own species, but also between different species.

> Both the dumb cattle and the races of wild beasts
> Are wont to utter different cries of varied sorts
> As they feel fear or pain, or as now joy prevails.
> [Lucretius V, 1058]

By a certain barking of a dog, a horse recognizes that he is angry; when he barks in another way the horse is not frightened. Even in animals which have no voice, from the coöperative services which we see them perform we readily infer some other means of communication: their movements are eloquent and expressive;

And this same principle is seen at work
When children gesture if they lack for words.
[Lucretius V, 1030]

Why should this not be so, just as our deaf mutes dispute, argue, and tell stories by signs? I have seen some so supple and so expert that in truth they reached full perfection in the art of making themselves understood. Lovers quarrel, are reconciled, entreat and thank one another, press their suit, and say in short all kinds of things with their eyes:

And even silence by itself
Can plead and speak.
[Tasso, *Aminta* II, 34]

And what about hands? We request, promise, call, dismiss, threaten, beg, supplicate, deny, refuse, question, admire, count, confess, repent, express fear, and shame, and doubt, instruct, command, incite, encourage, swear, testify, accuse, condemn, absolve, insult, disdain, challenge, spite, flatter, applaud, bless, humiliate, mock, reconcile, commend, exalt, celebrate, rejoice, complain, grieve, mourn, despair, express surprise, cry out, are still, and what not, with a variety and multiplicity which vie with the voice. With the head we summon, send away, avow, disavow, deny, welcome, honor, venerate, disdain, ask, dismiss, rejoice, lament, caress, scold, submit, defy, exhort, threaten, assure, inquire. What of the eyebrows? What of the shoulders? There is no movement which does not speak a language intelligible without study, and a language understood by all. In consequence, seeing its variety and wide use in contrast to other forms of expression, this language should rather be considered the proper one for man. I do not include what under special circumstances necessity teaches suddenly to those who have need of it, and finger alphabets, and gesture grammars, and the sciences which are practiced and expressed only through them, and the nations which Pliny says have no other language.

An ambassador of the city of Abdera, after talking a long time to King Agis of Sparta, asked him, "Well then, Sire, what answer do you wish me to take to our citizens?" "That I let you say all you wished, and talk as long as you wished, without ever saying a word myself." Wasn't that an expressive and readily understandable silence?

Intelligence of animals
and their social sense.

Moreover, what ability do we have which we do not recognize in the activities of animals? Is there a society governed with better order, diversified with more tasks and duties, and more constantly supervised, than that of honey-bees? Can we imagine that well-ordered arrangement of actions and assignments taking place without reasoning and without foresight?

> According to these signs and these examples,
> Some claim that bees share in the mind divine
> And in the emanations of the ether.
> [Virgil, *Georgics* IV, 219]

Do the swallows, which we see with the return of spring exploring all the corners of our houses, seek without judgment and choose without discretion from among a thousand sites the one which is the most suitable for the building of their house? And, in that beautiful and admirable organization of their structures, can birds use a square figure rather than a round, an obtuse angle in preference to a right angle, without knowing their conditions and effects? Do they sometimes take water, sometimes clay, without realizing that hardness is softened by moistening it? Do they line their palace with moss, or down, without foreseeing that the tender members of their young will be there more comfortable and more at ease? Do they cover themselves from the rainy wind, and turn their house toward the east, without knowing the different conditions of those winds and considering that one is for them more salutary than the other? Why does the spider thicken his web at one point and spin it finer at another? Why does it use now this sort of knot, now that one, if it does not deliberate, ponder, and draw conclusions? We recognize sufficiently, in most of their works, how much greater excellence animals have than we, and how inadequate our skill is to imitate them. We see, however, in our productions, less finished than theirs, the faculties which we employ in achieving them, and we recognize that our mind is using all its resources. Why do we not draw the same conclusion about them? Why do we attribute to I know not what natural and servile inclination works which surpass everything which we can achieve by nature and by art? In so doing, we attribute to them, without realizing it, a very great advantage over us, acknowledging that nature, with a motherly gentleness, accompanies and guides them, as by the hand, in all the events and situations of their life, while she abandons us to chance and fortune, and to seek by skill the things necessary for our preservation. At the same time she refuses us the means to be able to attain, by any instruction and effort of wits, the natural skill of beasts; so that their brutal stupidity surpasses in all situations anything which our divine intelligence can achieve.

*Man not inferior, but
one with the animals.*

Really, on this score, we should have good reason to call nature a most unjust stepmother. But it is not so at all; the order under which we live is not so formless and unregulated. Nature has taken care universally of all her creatures; there is none that she has not quite abundantly supplied with all the means necessary for the preservation of its being, for these common complaints which I hear men make (as the complete freedom of their opinions lifts them sometimes above the clouds, and then casts them down to the antipodes), that we are the only animal abandoned naked upon the naked earth, tied, bound, having nothing but the

skin of others to protect and clothe itself with, are un-
founded. They complain falsely that man is thus treated
while nature has covered all other creatures with shells,
pods, bark, hair, wool, quills, hide, bristles, feathers, scales,
fleece, or silk according to the need of their being; while
she has armed them with talons, teeth, horns for attack and
for defense; and while she herself has taught them what is
proper for them—to swim, to run, to fly, to sing—whereas
man can neither walk, nor speak, nor eat, nor do anything
but cry without a period of learning:

> The infant, like the sailor whom the furious waves
> Have cast upon the shore, naked and helpless lies
> On the bare ground; he cannot speak; indeed he lacks
> All aids to life as soon as from his mother's womb
> Into the realm of light harsh nature draws him forth.
> With plaintive wails he fills the air, as well befits
> One for whom life still holds in store so many woes.
> Quite otherwise grow up the farmyard's flocks and herds,
> And wild beasts, too. Their young need not be lulled and
>   soothed
> By rattles, and the tender nurse's whispered words.
> The changing seasons bring no need for different clothes,
> Nor need they arms nor battlements to guard their goods,
> For meeting all their wants the fertile earth itself,
> And nature's rich resources, unstintingly provide.
>   [Lucretius V, 222]

There prevail in the ordering of the universe a greater
equality and a more uniform provision.

Our skin is provided, as sufficiently as theirs, with
strength to withstand the inclemencies of the weather—
witness so many nations who have not yet experienced any
use of clothing. Our ancient Gauls were scarcely clad at all,
nor are the Irish, our neighbors, in so cold a climate. But
we can judge better by ourselves, for all parts of the body
which it pleases us to expose to the wind and air are capable
of enduring it: face, feet, hands, legs, shoulders, head, as
custom authorizes it. For, if there is a weak part in us, and

which seems to have to fear the cold, it ought to be the stomach where digestion takes place; our ancestors left it uncovered, and our ladies, soft and delicate as they are, sometimes go about with their garments half-open to the navel. The bindings and swaddling clothes of infants are not necessary, either, and mothers of Sparta raised theirs in complete liberty of movement of their limbs, without binding or restricting them. Our crying is common to most other animals too, and there are scarcely any which one does not see complain and whimper long after their birth: the more so since it is an attitude quite in keeping with the weakness which they feel in themselves. As for the action of eating, it is in us, as in them, natural and without instruction.

> For each feels his own strength upon which he can draw.
> [Lucretius V, 1033]

Who doubts that a child, having attained the strength to feed himself, would not know how to seek his food? And the earth produces and offers to him sufficient for his need, without further cultivation and tending; and if this is not so in all seasons, the situation is the same as for wild creatures. Consider the provisions which we see ants and others store up for the unproductive period of the year. Those nations which we have just discovered so abundantly provided with natural food and drink, without cultivation and without preparation, have recently made us aware that bread is not our only food, and that, without the effort of the plowman, our mother Nature had provided for us by planting everything we needed; indeed, as it is likely, more fully and more richly than she does now that we have taken a hand in it,

> At first the earth itself spontaneously brought forth
> For man the shining harvests and the fertile vine;
> She freely gave sweet fruits and pasture rich, which now,
> In spite of all our tilling, scarce produce at all;
> We wear our oxen out and sap our farmer's strength,
> [Lucretius II, 1157]

the uncontrolled excess of our appetite proceeding more rapidly than the inventions with which we seek to satisfy it.

As for weapons, we have received from nature more than most other animals, we have more varied movements of our members, and we draw greater use from them, naturally and without instruction. Those men who have become accustomed to fighting naked—one sees them rush into dangers just as our men do. If some beasts surpass us in this repect, we surpass many others. And we have by instinct and natural guidance the skill to fortify the body and cover it with borrowed materials. Similarly the elephant sharpens and grinds the teeth which he uses in fighting (for he has special ones for that purpose, which he spares and uses not at all for other ends). When bulls go into battle, they spread and throw dust about them; boars sharpen their tusks; and the ichneumon, when he must come to grips with the crocodile, protects his body, coats it and encrusts it all about with very dense and well-worked mud, as a coat of armor. Why should we not say that it is just as natural for us to arm ourselves with wood and iron?

As for speech, it is certain that if it is not natural it is not necessary. However, I think that a child who had been brought up in strict solitude, removed from all intercourse with others (which would be a very difficult experiment to carry out), would have some sort of speech to express his ideas. It is not believable that nature should have refused us this power which she has given various other animals: for what is it but speech, that faculty which we see them possess of complaining, rejoicing, calling for help, inviting one another to love, as they do by the use of their voice? How could it be that they not speak among themselves? They speak indeed to us, and we to them. In how many ways do we speak to our dogs? And they answer us. By other language, other forms of address, we distinguish them from birds, swine, cattle, horses, and change our idiom according to the species.

> Thus, amid their dark battalion, ants
> Accost each other, to inquire perhaps
> About their booty or their way.
> [Dante, *Purgatory* XXVI, 34]

It seems to me that Lactantius attributes to beasts not only speech but laughter as well. The difference in language which is seen among us, according to the regions where we dwell, is found also among animals of the same species. Aristotle cites in this connection the various songs of partridge according to the location,

> And certain birds
> Have different voices with the changing seasons,
> And some there are which, with a change in weather,
> Will modify their raucous cries.
> [Lucretius V, 1077, 1080, 1082, 1083]

But we do not know what sort of language a child raised alone would speak, and what is said about it as mere conjecture has little value. If, in order to attack my opinion, one brings up the fact that those born deaf do not speak, I answer that it is not only for not having been able to receive through the ear instruction in speaking, but rather because the sense of hearing, of which they are deprived, is related to the faculty of speech, and the two stand naturally combined: so that what we speak, we must first speak it to ourselves, and we must make it sound within our ears, before addressing it to others.

I have said all this to demonstrate the resemblance that there is between things animal and human, and to bring us down to join the ranks of all living creatures. We are neither above nor beneath the rest: everything that is under heaven, says the sage, is subject to a similar law and fortune:

> All things are bound by the chains of their own fate.
> [Lucretius V, 874]

There is some difference; there are orders and degrees; but it is all an integral part of the same nature:

soul

All things develop in their way, and all preserve
Essential differences which nature's changeless law
Long since decreed.

                    [Lucretius V, 921]

One must force man to take his place within the limits
of this order. The wretched being is unable, indeed, to step
outside them; he is hobbled and held, he is subject to the
same obligation as other creatures of his class, and he is of a
quite ordinary condition, without any prerogative, without
any real and essential superiority. The superiority which he
attributes to himself by pride and fancy has neither body
nor taste; and if it is true that he alone, of all animals, has
this liberty of imagination and this uncontrolled freedom of
thoughts, which represent to him what is, what is not, and
what he wishes, the false and the true, it is an advantage
which is sold to him at a high price and in which there is
very little reason for pride, for thence is born the principal
source of the evils which afflict him: sin, illness, irresolution,
confusion, despair.

*Intelligence of animals of
same nature as ours.*

I say then, to come back to my subject, that there is no
justification for considering that beasts do by natural and
inescapable inclination the same things which we do by our
choice and skill. We must conclude from similar effects
similar faculties, and confess in consequence that this same
reasoning, this same way which we insist we follow, belong
also to animals. Why do we imagine in them that natural
compulsion, we who feel no such effect ourselves? Besides,
it is more honorable to be led and obliged to act reasonably
by a natural and inevitable condition, and bears more resemblance to the divine, than to act reasonably through a rash
and fortuitous liberty; and it is safer to leave to nature
rather than to ourselves the reins of our conduct. The vanity
of our presumption makes us prefer to owe our sufficiency
to our own powers rather than to her liberality, and we

enrich the other animals with natural gifts and renounce them for ourselves in order to honor and ennoble ourselves with the gifts we painfully acquire. In this, it seems to me, we reveal a very simple turn of mind, for I shall certainly esteem as highly favors all mine and innate as those which I have had to go begging and seeking through experience. It is not in our power to acquire a finer recommendation than to be favored by God and nature.

Let us cite as an example the fox which the inhabitants of Thrace use when they wish to undertake crossing the ice of some frozen stream and which they release in front of them for that purpose. If we saw it at the edge of the stream cock its ear near the ice, to see whether it will hear the water flowing beneath at a greater or lesser distance, and as it finds the ice thicker or thinner draw back or advance, would it not be reasonable for us to conclude that there passes through its head the same reasoning which would take place in ours, and that it is a ratiocination and conclusion drawn from its natural sense: What makes a noise is moving; what moves is not frozen; what is not frozen is liquid, and yields under a weight? For to attribute that merely to keenness of hearing, without reasoning and drawing conclusions, is pure fancy and we cannot even imagine it. In the same way, we must consider so many sorts of ruses and tricks by which beasts protect themselves from the attacks which we undertake against them.

And if we wish to draw a feeling of superiority from the fact that we are able to seize them, use them, and make them obey our will, it is only that same power which we exercise over one another. We make slaves of men in a similar way. . . .

Diogenes, seeing his parents striving to buy his freedom from servitude, declared, "They are mad; it is the man who gives me food and lodging who serves me"; and those who look after animals must say rather that they serve them than they are served by them. . . .

So far as strength is concerned, there is no animal in

the world exposed to so many attacks as man; it doesn't take a whale, an elephant, and a crocodile, nor other such animals, a single one of which is capable of vanquishing a great number of men, to get the better of a man; fleas are sufficient to bring to a close Sulla's dictatorship; the heart and life of a great and triumphant emperor are the meal of a little worm. . . .

Moreover, the very share which we allow to animals in the favors of nature, by our own confession, is quite advantageous to them. We attribute to ourselves imaginary and fanciful gifts, future and absent possessions, concerning which it is not in our power to have any certainty, or possessions which we attribute to ourselves falsely through the unbridled freedom of our imagination—such gifts as reason, learning, and honor; and to animals we assign as their share essential goods, tangible and palpable—peace, repose, security, innocence, and health: health, I say, the most beautiful and richest present which nature can offer us. So true is this that philosophy, even Stoic philosophy, dares affirm that Heraclitus and Pherecydes, if they had been able to exchange their wisdom for health and by this bargain free themselves from the dropsy which afflicted one and the phthiriasis which tried the other, would have done well. In that conclusion these philosophers give even greater worth to wisdom than they do in this other proposition which is also theirs. They say that if Circe had presented to Ulysses two potions, one to turn a foolish man into a wise one, and the other a wise man into a foolish one, Ulysses ought rather to have accepted the potion of folly than to consent that Circe should change his human appearance into that of a beast; and they say that wisdom itself would have spoken to him in this way: "Abandon me, forget about me, rather than make me dwell within the countenance and form of a donkey." What! Philosophers will abandon that great and divine wisdom, then, preferring this corporeal and terrestrial garment? It is no longer, then, by reason, by mind, and by soul that we excel over beasts; it is by our beauty, our handsome complexion, and the fine proportion of our limbs. For them we must give up our intelligence, our prudence, and all the rest.

Now I accept this naïve and frank confession. Certainly they have recognized that those qualities in which we take such satisfaction are only a vain fancy. Even though beasts had, then, all Stoic virtue, knowledge, wisdom, and skill, they would still be beasts, nor could they be compared with a man, even a wretched, evil, and senseless one. In short, anything that is not as we are, is nothing worthwhile. And God himself, if he is to play an effective rôle, must make himself like us, as we shall see shortly! Whence it is clear that it is not by true reason, but by a mad and stubborn pride, that we prefer ourselves to other animals and hold ourselves aloof from their condition and their society.

CHAPTER III

The Futility of Learning

[*Summary*—Continuing his reply to the critics of Raymond Sebond by endeavoring to demonstrate the utter uselessness of all rational arguments, Montaigne asserts that the learning which the scholar painfully acquires is an empty and futile thing. It adds nothing to his health, his happiness, his well-being. Ignorance, indeed, is more effective than philosophy in helping us attain the end of tranquility and peace of mind. Madness, he declares, is akin to the agitations of the keenest intellect. True wisdom doubtless lies, as Socrates taught, in the recognition of one's ignorance. Montaigne presents at length and defends the attitude of the Skeptic who regards all things but suspends his judgment. He then presents the infinite contradictions of philosophic doctrines, and raises the question of the good faith of philosophers. Have they been less concerned with the truth than with displaying the fertile brilliance of their imagination? Among the gross blunders in the works of even the most noted philosophers, every conceivable fancy and fantasy is to be found. Truth is not attained by the vain efforts of the reason. It is a gift of God, through grace. In conclusion, Montaigne warns that while indeed the critic of Raymond Sebond may be defeated by such a demonstration of the inadequacy of the reason and the futility of learning, this weapon must be reserved cautiously for use as a last resort, for it involves abandoning your own weapons to make your opponent lose his. Under all usual circumstances, in argumentation as in living, be moderate and avoid extremes.]

Learning does not save us
from woes and torments.

But, to return to my subject, we have as part of our lot inconstancy, irresolution, incertitude, mourning, superstition, concern about things to come (even after our life), ambition,

34

avarice, jealousy, envy, appetites which are lawless, frenzied, and uncontrollable, war, falsehood, disloyalty, slander, and curiosity. Certainly we have paid strangely and dearly for that fine reason in which we glory, and that capacity to judge and know, if we have bought them at the price of this infinite number of passions to which we are a constant prey. That is, unless it still pleases us to insist, as Socrates does indeed, upon that notable prerogative over the other animals which we enjoy in that nature, whereas she has prescribed for them certain seasons and limits to sexual pleasure, has given us a free rein at all times and under all circumstances.

> "As wine is rarely good for invalids and is also most often harmful to them, so it is better not to give them any at all than to expose them to a manifest harm in the hope of a problematical advantage; so, perhaps, it would be better for mankind had nature refused us that activity of thought, that penetration, that industry which we call reason and which she has so liberally accorded us, since that activity is healthful to only a small number and fatal to all others."
>
> [Cicero, *De natura deorum* III, 27]

Of what profit can we consider that understanding of so many things to have been to Varro and Aristotle? Did it free them from the annoyances of human life? Were they spared the accidents which beset a common porter? Did they draw from logic some consolation for the gout? Because they knew how that humor settles in the joints, did they suffer any less from it? Were they reconciled with death for knowing that some nations rejoice at it, and with cuckoldry for knowing that in some regions wives are held in common? On the contrary, having held the highest rank for knowledge, one among the Romans and the other among the Greeks, and in the age when learning flourished most, we have not, however, learned that they had any special excellence in their lives; indeed the Greek is rather hard put to it to clear his name of certain noteworthy stains.

Has it been found that pleasure and health are more keenly enjoyed by one who knows astrology and grammar . . . and that shame and poverty are less a burden?

> Illness and weakness you will doubtless thus escape,
> And will be spared both grief and cares; a longer life
> And better fate will then be granted you.
>
> [Juvenal XIV, 156]

I have in my day seen a hundred artisans, a hundred peasants, wiser and happier than university rectors, and whom I should prefer to resemble. Scholarship, so I believe, has a place among the things necessary for life, like honor, nobility, dignity, or at most like beauty, wealth, and such other qualities which really contribute to it, but from afar, and somewhat more through imagination than by their essential value.

We need scarcely more services, rules, and laws of living, in our society, than cranes and ants do in theirs. And yet we see that they behave in a very well-ordered way without erudition. If man were wise, he would attribute to each thing its proper worth according as it was most useful and fitting for his life.

Virtue is born of humility
and submission.

Were one to judge us by our actions and excesses, there would be found a greater number of excellent men among the ignorant than among the learned, and I affirm it for every sort of virtue. Old Rome seems to me to have indeed borne men of greater worth, both for peace and for war, than that learned Rome which brought about its own ruin. Though in all other respects they might be equal, at least honesty and innocence would remain on the side of old Rome, for these qualities dwell singularly well with simplicity.

But I leave aside this reasoning, which would draw me farther than I should care to go. I shall merely reaffirm that it is only humility and submission which can produce a worthy man. One must not leave to the judgment of each person the recognition of his duty; it must be prescribed for him, not left for him to choose by the light of his own reason. Otherwise, according to the foolishness and infinite variety of our reasonings and opinions, we should end up by creating for ourselves duties which would result in our eating one another, as Epicurus says. The first law which God ever gave man was a law of pure obedience; it was a command, pure and simple, in which man had nothing to understand or discuss—appropriately so, since obedience is the principal function of a reasonable soul, recognizing a celestial superior and benefactor. From obedience and submission are born all other virtues, as from presumption is born all sin. And, on the other hand, the first temptation which came to human nature from the devil, his first poison, slyly entered our being through the promises which he gave us of understanding and knowledge: "Ye shall be as gods, knowing good and evil." [*Genesis* III, 5] And, in Homer, the sirens, to lure Ulysses and draw him into their dangerous and ruinous snares, offered him knowledge as a gift. The scourge of man is his claim to knowledge. That is why ignorance is so recommended to us by our religion as essential to belief and obedience. "Beware lest any man spoil you through philosophy and vain deceit, after . . . the rudiments of the world." [*Colossians* II, 8]

Presumption leads to vain boasting
about man's state and powers.

There is general agreement among all the philosophers of all schools that the sovereign good consists in tranquility of soul and body. But where do we find it?

> In short, the sage sees none above him save great Jove;
> For he is handsome, honored, rich, and free—indeed,
> The very king of kings; but most of all he knows
> Good health—unless he be afflicted with a cold.
> [Horace, Epistles I, i, 106]

It seems indeed that nature, to console us for our wretched
and puny state, has bestowed on us only presumption. That
is what Epictetus says—that man has nothing peculiarly his
own except the use he makes of his opinions. We have
received as our portion only wind and smoke. The gods
possess health as part of their essence, says philosophy, and
illness only in imagination; man, on the contrary, possesses
his gifts only in fancy, and his woes are part of his essence.
We have been right to insist upon the powers of our imagination, for all our blessings are only fanciful. Just hear the
boastings of this poor and calamity-stricken animal. "There
is nothing," says Cicero [*Tusculan Disputations* V, 36 and I,
26], "so pleasant as the pursuit of letters, those letters, I say,
by means of which the infinity of things, the immense greatness of nature, the very skies of this world, and the lands
and seas are revealed to us; it is they which have taught us
religion, moderation, greatness, and courage, and which
have snatched our soul away from darkness to show it all
things, the lofty and the low, the first and the last, and what
lies in between; it is they which furnish us what is necessary to live well and happily, and guide us to spend our life
without displeasure and harm." Does he not seem to be
speaking of the condition of the eternal and almighty God?

And so far as practice is concerned, a thousand unim-
portant women led in their village a life more equable, more
pleasant, and more consistent than was his.

> A god he was, indeed a very god, who found,
> O noble Memmius, that rule of life which now
> We call Philosophy, and by his wit and skill
> Gave life a firm foundation, quite secure from storms
> And such great darkness, and who brought it forth at last
> Into such great tranquility and such clear light.
>   [Lucretius V, 8]

These are quite magnificent and beautiful words; but a
very slight accident reduced the understanding of their

author[4] to a worse state than that of the meanest peasant, in spite of the teachings of that guiding god[5] and that divine wisdom. Of similar impudence is this promise of the book of Democritus: "I am going to talk to you about all things" [Cicero, *Academica* II, 23]; and this stupid title which Aristotle bestows on us, calling us "mortal gods"; and the judgment of Chrysippus, that Dion was as virtuous as God. And my Seneca recognized, he says, that God had given him life, but that he himself was responsible for living well; this is in keeping with another dictum: "With reason do we pride ourselves upon our virtue, which would not be the case if we held it as a gift from God, and not through our own efforts." [Cicero, *De natura deorum* III, 36] This is also from Seneca: that the wise man has fortitude comparable to God's, but in the midst of human weakness; and for that reason he surpasses God. There is nothing so ordinary as to encounter remarks of such rashness. There is none of us who takes such offense at seeing himself exalted to the level of God as he does at seeing himself pushed back to the level of the other animals: so much more jealous are we of our own interest than of our creator's.

But we must trample down that foolish vanity, and sharply and boldly overthrow the ridiculous foundations on which these false opinions are built. So long as he thinks he has some freedom of action and some power in himself, man will never recognize what he owes to his master; he will always count his chickens before they are hatched, as they say; he must be stripped of all but his shirt.

Let us see a few noteworthy examples of the effect of this philosophy.

Posidonius, being afflicted with such a painful illness that it made him wring his hands and gnash his teeth, thought that he was defying pain by crying out to it: "It

---

[4] Tradition has it that Lucretius went insane.
[5] Epicurus.

does you no good to rack me, if I do not admit that you are hurting me." He feels the same emotions as my servant, but he boasts because he at least holds his tongue according to the laws of his philosophic school. "It was not proper to be boastful in speech, but to yield in fact." [Cicero, *Tusculan Disputations* II, 13]

Arcesilaus was ill with the gout; Carneades, having come to visit him and going away deeply afflicted, Arcesilaus called him back and, pointing first to his feet and then his chest: "What bothers me there," he said to him, "has not affected me here." He has somewhat better grace, for he recognizes that he is suffering and would like to be rid of his infirmity; but his heart, however, has not been overwhelmed and weakened by it. The other maintains his inflexibility, more verbal, in my opinion, than real. And Dionysius of Heraclea, afflicted with a great burning sensation in his eyes, was induced thereby to abandon these Stoic resolves.

*Ignorance aids more than knowledge
in enduring misfortunes.*

But even though learning should achieve what they say, blunting and reducing the bitterness of the misfortunes which pursue us, what does it do that in a more direct and more obvious way ignorance doesn't do? The philosopher Pyrrho, undergoing at sea the hazard of a great storm, presented to those who were with him, as an example to imitate, only the security of a pig that was traveling with them and that looked out on the storm without fright. Philosophy, finding its precepts useless, refers us to the example of an athlete and a mule-driver, in whom one sees ordinarily much less fear of death, of pain, and of other troubles, and more steadfastness than learning ever furnished to anyone who wasn't born to it and prepared for it himself by natural habit. What brings it about that one makes an incision and cuts the tender members of a child more readily than ours, unless it is ignorance? And what about those of a horse? How many have been made ill by the mere force of imagination? We customarily see people bled, purged, and doctored in order to cure ills which they feel only in their minds. When we lack real ills, our learning lends us its own. This color and complexion indicate that you will have some catarrhal discharge; this hot season threatens you with a feverish disturbance; this break in the life line of your left hand warns you of some important illness about to come. And finally imagination turns destructively upon good health itself. That animation and vigor of youth cannot remain stable; we must remove some of their blood and strength lest they turn against you. Compare the life of a man subjected to such imaginations with that of a peasant letting himself go according to his natural inclination, measuring things only by the way he feels at the moment, without science, and without foreseeing woes to come, who has illness only when it actually strikes him. In contrast, the other one often has the stone in his mind before he has it in his kidneys; as if it were not soon enough to suffer illness when it is at hand, he anticipates it in imagination, and hastens to meet it.

What I say about medicine can in general be drawn by example from any field of learning. Thus arose that former opinion of philosophers who placed the supreme good in the recognition of the weakness of our judgment. My ignorance gives me as much occasion for hope as for fear, and having no other rule for my health than that of the examples of others and of the events which I see elsewhere in similar circumstances, I find all kinds of them and accept the comparisons which are most favorable to me. I receive health with open arms, free, full, and complete, and sharpen my appetite to enjoy it—all the more so since it is now less ordinary and more rare; far be it from me that I should disturb its repose and its gentleness by the bitterness of a new and restricted manner of living. Animals show us sufficiently how many diseases the agitation of our minds brings to us.

They tell us of the people of Brazil that they died only of old age, and they attribute it to the serenity and tranquility of their air. I attribute it rather to the tranquility and serenity of their soul, freed of all passion and care, and of all tense or unpleasant concern, as people who spent their life in an admirable simplicity and ignorance, without letters, without law, without a king, without any religion whatsoever.

And how does it happen, for this is shown by experience, that the roughest and dullest are the most sure and most desirable in the act of love, and that the love of a muledriver becomes often more acceptable than that of a gentleman, unless it be that in the latter the agitation of the mind disturbs his bodily strength, breaks it, and wears it out?

*Keenness of intellect
and madness related.*

For the mind customarily wearies and disturbs itself. What maddens it, drives it more commonly into derangement, than its own liveliness, its keenness, and in short its very force? What is the source of the most subtle folly, if not the most subtle wisdom? As from great friendships grow great enmities, from vigorous health mortal illnesses, so from the rare and vigorous agitations of our minds are born the most excellent and completely unbalanced manias; it takes just a half-turn of the tuning peg to pass from one to the other. By the actions of madmen, we see how closely allied madness is with the most vigorous operation of our mind. Who does not know how nearly imperceptible is the borderline between madness and the vigorous elevations of a free mind, or between madness and the effects of a supreme and extraordinary virtue? Plato says that those of melancholy temperament are the most readily taught and most excellent; and so there are none who have so great a propensity to insanity. Minds of broadest scope are ruined by their own force and suppleness. What fate has just befallen, through his own agitation and eagerness, an Italian poet,[6] one of the most judicious, ingenious, and most thoroughly imbued with the spirit of ancient and pure poetry that his country has seen in a long time? Does he not have reason to be grateful to that destructive keenness of his mind? To that light which has blinded him? To that exact and strained capacity of his reason which has left him without reason? To the meticulous and painstaking pursuit of learning which has led him to insanity? To that rare aptitude for activities of the intelligence, which has left him without activity and without intelligence? I felt even more vexation than compassion, seeing him at Ferrara in such a pitiful state, surviving himself, not knowing either himself or his works which, without his knowledge, and yet before his very eyes, were published without being corrected and put in shape.

Do you wish a healthy man? Do you wish him to be balanced, and of a sure and firm equilibrium? Let him be wrapped in darkness, idleness, and dullness. We must become stupid to be wise, and blinded to be led.

Well-being is but freedom
from pain.

And if they tell me that the advantage of feeling suffering and pain in a cold and blunted way brings as a consequence the disadvantage of making us also less keen and perceptive for the enjoyment of good things and pleasures, that is true; but the misery of our condition brings it about that we have less to enjoy than to flee, and that extreme pleasure moves us less than a slight pain. "Men are less sensitive to pleasure than to pain." [Livy XX, 21] We do not feel complete health as we do the least of illnesses.

---

[6] Torquato Tasso (1544-1595), distinguished Italian poet.

> Our body feels
> The slightest blows which barely brush the skin,
> While it remains unconscious of good health.
> In this alone I find cause to rejoice—
> That neither chest nor foot torments me now.
> Indeed, scarce otherwise is man aware
> That he's in health and well.
>   [Lines by La Boétie, Montaigne's closest friend]

Our well-being is only freedom from pain. That is why the philosophical school which has given the greatest importance to pleasure has also reduced it to mere absence of pain. Not to suffer is the greatest good that man can hope for. . . . For that very tingling and quickening which is experienced in certain pleasures and which seems to raise us above simple health and lack of pain, that pleasure which is active, moving, and (how shall I put it?) burning and sharp, even it aims only at absence of discomfort as its goal. The appetite which drives us to intercourse with women seeks only to drive away the trouble which burning and furious desire brings to us, and asks only to be appeased, and left at rest, and freed from that fever. And so with others, too.

I say, then, that if simplicity leads us to have no pain, it leads us to a very happy state, in view of our human lot.

And yet one must not imagine that apathy so leaden that it destroys all feeling. For Crantor was right to combat the apathy of Epicurus if one made it so deep that the very approach and birth of sufferings were not felt. I do not praise such an apathy, which is neither possible nor desirable. I am happy not to be ill; but if I am ill, I want to know that I am; and if they cauterize or cut me, I want to feel it. Truly, were one to root out the recognition of pain, one would eliminate at the same time all sense of pleasure, and finally would destroy man: "This insensibility can be acquired only at a high price—spiritual dullness and corporal torpor." [Cicero, *Tusculan Disputations* III, 6] Suffering, in its due turn, is part of man's lot. Pain is not always to be avoided, nor pleasure always to be sought.

*Philosophy counsels a cowardly
retreat from adversities.*

It is a great contribution to the honor of ignorance that science itself pushes us into its arms when it is incapable of stiffening us against the weight of misfortunes; she is obliged to accept that compromise, to give us free rein, and to give us leave to escape into the embrace of ignorance and to seek under its protection a shelter from the blows and insults of fortune. What else does she mean when she advises us to turn our mind away from the troubles which beset us, and to divert it with the recollection of vanished pleasures, and to use, in order to console ourselves for present ills, the memory of past delights, and to call to our aid a vanished contentment in order to oppose it to what is weighing upon us—"in order to relieve troubles, he (Epicurus) advises turning the mind away from any bothersome thought and directing it to the contemplation of pleasant memories" [Cicero, *Tusculan Disputations* III, 15]—if not that, when she lacks power, she intends to use trickery, and by a twist and a kick make up for the strength of body and arms which have failed her? For, not merely for a philosopher, but even for any reasonable man, when he feels a burning thirst as a consequence of a fever, are you not shortchanging him when you pay him with the recollection of the coolness of Greek wine? It would rather make his situation worse, for

He who remembers good times redoubles his sorrow.
[Based on Dante, *Inferno* V, 121]

The same can be said about this other counsel which philosophy gives, to retain in memory only past happiness, and to erase the unpleasant experiences which we have suffered—as if we had in our power the art of forgetting. Once again, that is a counsel which reduces our worth. "Sweet is the memory of past troubles." [Cicero, *De finibus* I, 17]

How does philosophy, which ought to arm me to face fate and strengthen my courage to triumph over all human adversities, descend to that weakness of making me slink away through recourse to these cowardly and ridiculous devices? For memory brings before us, not what we choose, but what it pleases. Indeed, there is nothing which impresses so vividly something in our memory as the desire to forget it: a good way to store safely and to impress something in our mind is to seek to make the memory reject it. This statement is false: "It lies within us to bury as it were in perpetual oblivion our misfortunes, and to recall cheerful and pleasant memories of happy times." [Cicero, *De finibus* I, 17] And this one is true: "I remember even what I do not wish to, and I cannot forget what I would." [Cicero, *De finibus* II, 32] And who gives this advice? He "who alone dared proclaim himself wise," [Cicero, *De finibus* II, 3, speaking of Epicurus]

> Who by his genius has surpassed all humankind,
> As rising in the heavens the sun outshone the stars.
> [Lucretius III, 1043]

To empty and vacate the memory, is that not the true and right road to ignorance? "Ignorance is an ineffective remedy against evils." [Seneca, *Oedipus* III, 17] We encounter numerous similar precepts by which we are permitted to borrow from the common people frivolous attitudes when keen and strong reason is not effective enough, provided they bring us contentment and consolation. Where we cannot heal the wound, they are content to deaden it and to use palliatives. I believe that they will not deny me this, that if they could, by means of some weakness and illness of judgment, add order and constancy to a state of life which is maintained in pleasure and tranquility, they would accept it:

> By drinking and by strewing flowers shall I begin,
> Though I be taken for a fool. . . .
> [Horace, *Epistles* I, v, 14]

Pride is man's ruin.

Christians know especially well what a natural and original evil curiosity is in man. The effort to increase in wisdom and in knowledge was the original cause of the downfall of the human race; it is the road which led it headlong to eternal damnation. Pride is its ruin and its corruption: it is pride which persuades man to turn aside from the common paths, which makes him embrace new things, and prefer to be the leader of a troop wandering and lost on the road to perdition, prefer to be a master and teacher of error and falsehood rather than to be a disciple in the school of truth, letting himself be led and guided by another's hand along the beaten path and the straight way. . . .

O presumption! How you trip us up! After Socrates was informed that the god of wisdom had proclaimed him a wise man, he was astonished at it; and, examining himself and seeking in all his person, he found there no justification for that divine proclamation. He knew men as just, temperate, courageous, learned, as himself, and more eloquent, and more handsome, and more useful to the state. Finally he came to the conclusion that he was distinguished from the others and was wise only because he did not consider himself so; and that his god deemed it a peculiar stupidity in man to pride himself on learning and wisdom; and that his best doctrine was the doctrine of ignorance, and his best wisdom, simplicity.

The Holy Bible declares that those among us who have a high opinion of themselves are wretched. "Dust and ashes," it says to them, "what reason have you to glorify yourselves?" And elsewhere, "God has made man like a shadow; concerning which who shall judge when, the light having been taken away, it will have vanished?" We are indeed nothing. So far are our capacities from conceiving the loftiness of God that, of the works of our creator, those best bear his mark and are best his which we understand the least. To encounter an unbelievable thing is for Christians an occasion to believe. It is all the more according to reason as it is against human reason. If it were according to reason, it would no longer be a miracle; and if it followed some example, it would no longer be a unique thing. "God is better known when one knows him not," says St. Augustine [*De ordine* II, 16]; and Tacitus: "It is more holy and reverent to believe concerning the acts of the gods than to know." [*De Germania* XXXIV] And Plato considers that there is some vice of impiety in too searchingly inquiring about God, and the world, and the first causes of things. . . .

We say indeed "power," "truth," "justice": those are words which signify something great; but that thing itself, we do not see it at all nor do we conceive it. We say that God fears, that God grows angry, that God loves,

> Expressing things divine in mortal terms;
> [Lucretius V, 122]

those are all agitations and emotions which cannot be in God as we know them; nor can we imagine them in his way. Only God alone can know and interpret his works. And he does so in our language, inexactly, in order to demean himself and descend to us who are upon the ground, groveling. How can prudence be a quality of his nature, for prudence is the choice between good and evil, and no evil touches him? What do reason and intelligence, which we use in order to arrive at obvious things from obscure ones, have to do with him, since there is nothing obscure for God? Justice, which distributes to each what belongs to him, is engendered by the society and community of men; how, then, can it be in God? What about temperance, which is moderation in bodily pleasures, when these have no place in the divine? Fortitude to endure pain, effort, dangers, belongs to him just as little, these three things never approaching him. Therefore Aristotle considers him likewise exempt from virtue and vice. "He is incapable of affection, or anger, because such passions are found only in weak beings." [Cicero, *De natura deorum* I, 17]

The highest knowledge cannot be attained by reason.

It is not by our own efforts that we have acquired whatever share we may have in the knowledge of the truth. God has made that sufficiently clear by the witnesses which he has chosen among the common, simple, and ignorant people to instruct us in his admirable secrets: our faith is not something we have acquired—it is a pure gift from another's liberality. It is not by reasoning or by our understanding that we have received our religion; it is by an authority and a command outside ourselves. The weakness of our judgment aids us more to accept it than does its strength, and our blindness more than our vision. It is through our ignorance rather than our knowledge that we are learned in this divine learning. It is no marvel if our natural and earthly faculties cannot conceive that supernatural and celestial knowledge: let us bring to it of our own merely obedience and submissiveness. For, as it is written, "I will destroy the wisdom of the wise, and I will bring to nothing the understanding of the prudent. Where is the wise? Where is the scribe? Where is the disputer of this world? Hath not God made foolish the wisdom of this world? For after that in the wisdom of God the world by wisdom knew not God, it pleased God by the foolishness of preaching to save them that believe." [I *Corinthians* I, 19]

And so I must see finally whether it is in the power of man to find what he seeks, and if that quest which he has pursued for so many centuries has enriched him with some new strength and some solid truth.

I believe that he will confess to me, if he speaks conscientiously, that the sole profit which he has drawn from such a long pursuit is to have learned to recognize his weakness. The ignorance which was by nature in us, we have by a long study confirmed and verified it. There has happened to truly learned people what happens to heads of wheat: they go rising and mounting, with heads held high and proud, so long as they are empty; but when they are full and swollen with grain in their maturity, they begin to bend in humility and to bow their heads. Likewise, men having tested and probed everything, having found in this accumulation of learning and this stock of so many various things nothing substantial and solid, and nothing but vanity, they have given up their presumption and recognized their natural condition. . . .

It will be really too easy if I consider man as commonly formed and in general, and yet I might well do so by his own rule which judges the truth, not by the worth of those expressing a judgment, but by their number. Let us leave aside the ordinary man

> Who even snores while he's awake . . . and so for whom,
> Living and seeing, life's already close to death,
>
> [Lucretius III, 1048 and 1046]

who is not aware of himself, who does not judge himself, who leaves idle most of his natural faculties. I wish to take man at the loftiest point he has attained. Let us consider him in that small number of excellent and select men who, having been endowed with fine and special natural powers, have strengthened and sharpened them carefully even more, through study and skill, and have raised them to the highest degree of wisdom which they can reach. In their probings, they have taken their mind back and forth, and to and fro; they have strengthened and buttressed it with all the outside help proper to it, and enriched and adorned it with everything they could borrow for its advantage from within and without the world; it is within them that resides the extreme summit of human nature. They have established for the world societies and laws; they have taught it through arts and sciences, and even more by the example of their admirable lives. I shall consider only those persons, their testimony and their experience. Let us see how far they have gone and to what they have held fast. The infirmities and defects which we shall find in that select body, the world can boldly accept as its own.

Skepticism is the attitude of those
who continue to seek the truth.

Whoever seeks something, comes to this point: either he says that he has found it, or that it can't be found, or that he is still pursuing his quest. All philosophy is divided into these three types. Its goal is to seek truth, knowledge, and certitude. Peripatetics, Epicureans, Stoics, and others have thought they had reached that goal. These philosophers established the fields of learning which we now know, and treated them as things known for a certainty. Clitomachus, Carneades, and the followers of the Academy gave up hope in their search, and concluded that the truth could not be grasped by our faculties. They find at the end of their quest weakness and human ignorance. This school has had the greatest following and the noblest disciples.

Pyrrho and other Skeptics or Ephectic philosophers, whose doctrines numerous ancients thought to be drawn from Homer, the seven sages, Archilochus, and Euripides (and they include with them Zeno, Democritus, Xenophanes), say that they are still seeking the truth. They judge that those who think they have found it are completely mistaken, and that there is still too bold a vanity in the second category of philosophers who assure that human powers are not capable of attaining it. For to establish the measure of our capabilities, to know and judge the difficulty of things—that is a great and prodigious science, which they doubt lies within man's powers.

> Now if one thinks that nothing can be known,
> That very fact he cannot know for sure,
> For he proclaims he knows not anything.
> [Lucretius IV, 469]

Ignorance which recognizes itself, which judges and which condemns itself, is not a complete ignorance: to be so, it must be unaware of itself. So that the profession of the Pyrrhonians is to shake the foundations of belief, to doubt, and to inquire, to be assured of nothing, to answer for nothing. Of the three actions of the soul—the imaginative, the appetitive, and the consenting—they accept only the first two; the last, they keep it and maintain it in a state of balance, wihout any inclination or approval, however slight, to one side or the other. . . .

*The Skeptic suspends
his judgment.*

Now this attitude of their judgment, rigid and inflexible, receiving all objects without judgment and consent,
leads them to their *ataraxia,* a condition of life which is
peaceful, calm, free from the agitations which come to us
through the impression of the idea and the knowledge which
we think we have of things. From that impression are born
fear, avarice, envy, immoderate desires, ambition, pride, superstition, love of novelty, rebellion, disobedience, stubbornness, and most bodily ills. They even free themselves
thus from jealousy about their teaching, for they debate only
in a very mild way. They do not fear rebuttal to their argument. When they say that what has weight goes downward,
they would be quite sorry to be believed; they seek to be
contradicted, in order to arouse doubt and the suspension of
judgment, for that is their goal. They advance their propositions only in order to combat the ones they think we have
in our belief. If you adopt the view they have been defending, they will as readily take the other side: it all one to
them, for they make no choice. . . . By this extreme doubt,
which shakes even its own foundations, they keep themselves apart from several schools, even from those very ones
which have taught in various ways doubt and ignorance. . . .

Where others are driven as by a storm, either by the
custom of their country, or the training received at home, or
by chance, without judgment and without choice, indeed
most often before the age of discretion, to such or such an
opinion, to the Stoic or Epicurean schools, to which they
find themselves indentured, enslaved, and attached as if they
cannot let go—"to some school or other, as if cast ashore by
a storm, to it as to a rock they cling"—why should it not
likewise be granted these Skeptics to maintain their liberty,
and to consider things without obligation and servitude—
"all the more free and independent because their faculty of
judgment is unencumbered?" [Cicero, *Academica* II, 3] Is it

not some advantage to be freed of the necessity which restricts the others? Is it not better to remain in suspense than to be entangled in the multitude of errors which human imagination has produced? Is it not better to be uncommitted than to be involved in those seditious and quarrelsome conflicts? "But what will I choose?—Whatever you like, so long as you make a choice." That's a stupid answer, but it seems however that all dogmatism eventually comes to it, not permitting us to be ignorant of what we do not know. Take the most famous doctrine; it will never be so certain that, to defend it, you won't have to attack and combat a hundred and a hundred contrary doctrines. Is it not better to stand apart from this struggle? It is permissible for you to espouse, as your honor and your life, the belief of Aristotle about the eternity of the soul, and to deny and contradict Plato on that point, and yet it will be forbidden the Skeptics to remain in doubt concerning it? If it is permissible for Panaetius to suspend his judgment concerning divinations, dreams, oracles, vaticinations, which for the Stoics are not subject to any doubt, why should a sage not venture in all things what this one dares in regard to things which he has learned from his masters, established with the common consent of the school whose teachings he accepts and professes? . . .

The Pyrrhonians speak thus: I establish nothing. It is no more this way than that way, nor is it neither one nor the other; I do not understand it; evidence is equal on all sides; it is equally legitimate to speak for or against. Nothing seems true which may not also seem false. Their ritualistic word is επέχω, that is to say, "I suspend judgment, I don't lean one way or the other." Those are their refrains, and others of similar substance. Their effect is a pure, complete, and perfect postponement and suspension of judgment. They use their reason to question and to debate, but not to conclude and to choose. Whoever will imagine a perpetual confession of ignorance, a judgment without propensity or inclination, on whatever occasion it may be, will have a clear picture of Pyrrhonism. I express this idea as clearly as I can, for many find it difficult to imagine, and even the authors of it present it somewhat obscurely and variously.

As far as the activities of life are concerned, they behave much as other people. They lend and accommodate themselves to natural inclinations, to the impulse and constraint of passions, to the established laws and customs, and to the tradition of the arts. "For God willed, not that we should know those things, but merely that we might use them." [Cicero, *De divinatione* I, 18] They let their common actions be guided by those things, without offering an opinion or forming a judgment. As a consequence, I cannot make what they say about Pyrrho jibe with this principle. They depict him as dull and unfeeling, adopting an untamed and anti-social manner of living, standing in the way of carts or at the edge of precipices, refusing to conform to laws. That is a gross exaggeration of his teaching. He had no wish to make of himself a stone or a stump; he wanted to make of himself a living man, using his mind and reason, enjoying all pleasures and natural satisfactions, putting to service and utilizing all his bodily and spiritual faculties in a disciplined and honorable way. As for the fanciful privileges, imaginary and false, which man has usurped, and which give him power to govern, regulate, and establish the truth—in good faith he renounced and abandoned them.

*Philosophers enjoy speculation
on inconsequential and
impenetrable subjects.*

Aristotle piles up for us ordinarily a great number of other opinions and other beliefs to compare with his own and to show us how far he has advanced beyond them, and how much closer he has come to verisimilitude. Truth, after all, is not judged by the authority and testimony of others. And therefore Epicurus carefully avoided citing others' opinions in his writings. Aristotle is the prince of dogmatic philosophers; and yet we learn from him that great knowledge provides the occasion for greater doubt. One sees him deliberately cover himself often with an obscurity so dense and impenetrable that one cannot discover through it anything about his own opinion. This is in effect a Pyrrhonism under a dogmatic disguise. . . .

Chrysippus used to say that what Plato and Aristotle had written about logic had been written as a game and exercise, and he could not believe that they had spoken with conviction about so vain a subject. Plutarch speaks in the same way about metaphysics. Epicurus would have done so also about rhetoric, grammar, poetry, mathematics, and, except for physics, about all the sciences. And Socrates concerning all, also, except that one which deals with morals and life. No matter what one made inquiry about, he would always first of all induce his questioner to give an account of the conditions of his life, present and past, which he examined and judged, considering any other preliminaries subordinate to that and superfluous.

"That learning which has in no way contributed to the virtue of those who have taught it pleases me little." [Sallust, 85] Most of the arts have thus been disdained by learned men themselves. But they did not consider that it was inappropriate to exercise and amuse their minds in matters where there was nothing worthwhile and substantial.

Moreover, some have considered Plato a dogmatic philosopher; others, a Skeptic; still others, in some things one, and in some things the other. . . .

Democritus, having eaten at his table figs which had a flavor of honey, began suddenly to seek in his mind whence that unusual sweetness came to them and, to enlighten himself on the subject, was going to rise from the table to examine the situation of the place where the figs had been gathered. His maid, having heard the cause of this moving about, laughingly told him that he shouldn't trouble himself on that account, for the fact was that she had put them in a dish where there had been honey. He was annoyed that she had taken from him the occasion for that research, and robbed his curiosity of a problem. "Look," he said to her, "You have annoyed me; I shall nevertheless not give up seeking the cause as if it were natural." And deliberately he succeeded in finding some real reason for a false and imaginary effect. This story of a famous and great philosopher shows to us very clearly that studious passion by which we find amusement in the pursuit of things which we have no hope of discovering. Plutarch tells a similar story about someone who did not wish to be enlightened about something which was perplexing him so that he might not lose the pleasure of seeking the solution; as that other man who did not wish his doctor to take from him the thirst induced by fever, so as not to lose the pleasure of quenching it by drinking. "It is better to learn useless things than to learn nothing." [Seneca, *Epistles* 88]

Just as in our eating there is often nothing but pleasure, and as everything we eat which is pleasant is not always nutritious or healthful, so likewise what our mind draws from learning does not fail to be a source of pleasure, even though it too may not be nourishing or salutary.

Here is what they say. The study of nature is a food fit for our minds; it elevates and broadens us, makes us disdain low and earthly things by the comparison with higher and celestial things. The very seeking of hidden and great things is most pleasant, even to him who acquires thereby an attitude of reverence and a fear of passing judgment. Those are adages of their profession. The vain image of this sickly curiosity is seen more precisely still in this other example which they quote so often and with high approval. Eudoxus wished and prayed the gods that he might once see the sun at close range, understand its form, its greatness, and its beauty, at the price of being himself straightway consumed by fire. He wishes, at the cost of his life, to acquire a knowledge the use and possession of which will be immediately taken from him, and, for this sudden and fleeting knowledge, lose all other knowledge which he has and which he might subsequently acquire.

*Ingenious novelty the aim
of much philosophy.*

I can't really convince myself that Epicurus, Plato, and Pythagoras have given us as real coin of the realm their atoms, their ideas, and their numbers. They were too wise to establish their articles of faith on something so uncertain and so debatable. But, in this obscurity and ignorance of the world, each of these great personages strove to bring some suggestion of light, and they directed their intelligence to inventions which might have at least a clever and pleasant appearance, if only, however false, they could be defended against contrary presentations: "Each draws these ideas from his imagination, and not from the strength of his knowledge." [Seneca, *Suasoriae* IV] A man of antiquity who was reproached with professing philosophy while in his personal judgment he didn't think much of it, answered that that was truly philosophizing. They wanted to consider everything, weigh everything, and they thought that occupation in keeping with the natural curiosity which is within us. Some things they wrote for the need of the society of their state, such as their religious writings. In this they were reasonable, because they did not wish to rip apart public beliefs and thus sought to avoid giving rise to disturbances regarding obedience to the laws and customs of their country.

Plato treats this mystery by means of a rather obvious device. For, when he presents his own beliefs, he imposes nothing as certain. When he plays the rôle of lawmaker, he borrows a pedantic and assertive style, and mingles boldly there the most fantastic of his inventions, as useful when one persuades the public to accept them as they are ridiculous when we accept them ourselves. Plato realized how prone we are to accept all ideas and, above all, the wildest and most fanciful.

And therefore, in his *Laws*, he is most careful to decree

that there may be sung in public only poems whose imaginative fictions tend to some useful end; and since it is so easy to impress all myths in the human mind, he held that it is an injustice not to feed it on profitable lies rather than on useless or harmful lies. He says quite explicitly in his *Republic* that, for their own benefit, it is often necessary to deceive men. . . .

There are other subjects which they have sifted and tossed, one to the left, one to the right, each striving, with reason or without, to give them an appearance of something new. For, having found nothing so hidden but they wished to talk of it, they are often obliged to set forth weak and absurd conjectures, not that they have taken them themselves as a starting point, nor to build some truth upon them, but for the exercise of their ingenuity. . . .

*Our reason cannot know God
nor understand creation.*

And, if one did not view the matter thus, how should we explain such a great inconstancy, variety, and vanity of opinions as we see that these excellent and admirable minds have produced? For, to take one example, what is more vain that to seek to imagine God according to our analogies and conjectures, to subject him and the universe to rules of human measure and to our laws, and to use at the expense of the divinity this little fragment of reason which it has pleased him to bestow upon our nature? And, because we cannot extend our range of vision as far as his glorious abode, to have brought him down to our corruption and our miseries?

Of all the opinions of men of antiquity concerning religion, that one seems to me to have had the highest degree of probability and the best justification which recognized God as an incomprehensible power, source and preserver of all things, all goodness, all perfection, receiving and accepting the honor and reverence which human beings rendered him, no matter in what guise, name, and manner:

Almighty Jupiter, father and mother
Of all creation, of kings and gods themselves. . . .
[Valerius Soranus, quoted by St. Augustine,
City of God VII, xi]

Pythagoras vaguely suggested the truth more closely, judging that the knowledge of this first cause and being of beings must be indefinite, without definition, without description; that it was nothing other than the extreme effort of our imagination toward perfection, each amplifying the idea according to his capacity. But if Numa undertook to make the worship of his people conform to this conception, to make it part of a purely intellectual religion, addressed to a vague, unknowable deity and without any material admixture, he was undertaking a useless thing; the human mind cannot remain floating in that vague infinity of shapeless thoughts; it must bring them together into a definite image made according to its own likeness. Divine majesty has thus let itself for us be somewhat circumscribed within corporal limits; its supernatural and celestial sacraments bear marks of our terrestrial condition; its worship is expressed through rites and words which appeal to the senses; for it is man who believes and who prays. I leave aside the other arguments which are used on this subject. But one can scarcely make me believe that the sight of our crucifixes and the depiction of that sorrowful torment, that the ceremonial ornaments and movements of our worship, that the voices matching the devotion of our thought, and that all this appeal to the senses, do not warm the soul of the populace with a religious passion of very useful effect. . . .

It has always seemed to me that for a Christian it is highly improper and irreverent to speak as follows: God cannot die; God cannot contradict himself; God cannot do this or that. I do not think it is fitting to restrict thus the divine power beneath the laws of our speech. And we should present more reverently and more religiously the concept which these propositions offer us.

Our speech has its weaknesses and its faults, as all the

rest. Most of the sources of the disorders in the world are grammatical. Our lawsuits are born only out of the debate concerning the interpretation of the laws; and most wars, out of the inability involved in not knowing how to express clearly the conventions and treaties of agreement of princes. How many quarrels, and what important ones, have been produced in the world by doubt concerning the meaning of this syllable: *hoc!* . . . I see the Pyrrhonian philosophers who cannot express their general conception in any manner of speaking, for they would need a new language. Ours is all formed of affirmative propositions, to which they are completely opposed. As a consequence, when they say: "I doubt," people immediately seize them by the throat to make them confess that at least they affirm and know that much, that they doubt. . . .

That notion is more adequately expressed in the form of a question: "What do I know?", as I bear it as a motto along with the image of a balance. . . .

When we say that the infinite number of centuries, both past and future, are to God only an instant; that his goodness, wisdom, power are one with his essence, our words declare it, but our intelligence does not understand it. And yet our presumption wishes to sift the divine through our sieve. And from that are born all the fanciful ideas and errors which this world has seized upon, bringing to its balance and weighing therein something so remote from its measure. "It is a marvel how far the arrogance of the human heart goes, encouraged by the slightest success." [Pliny, II, 23]

May it please nature one day to open her bosom and to reveal to us as they are the means and operation of its movements, and to prepare our eyes for that revelation! O God! What errors, what misconceptions we should find in our poor science! I am mistaken if science has grasped a single thing correctly; and I shall leave here ignorant of everything except my ignorance.

*The teachings of philosophy are
mere poetic speculations.*

Have I not read in Plato this divine remark, that nature
is nothing but an enigmatic poem? As perhaps one might
say a veiled and obscure painting, gleaming with an infinite
variety of reflections to invite our conjectures. "All those
things are enveloped and hidden in thick darkness, and
there is nothing in the human mind sharp enough to penetrate to heaven and to probe into the depths of the earth."
[Cicero, *Academica* II, 39]

And certainly philosophy is only a sophisticated poetry.
Where do those ancient authors draw all their authorities if
not from poets? And the first philosophers were poets themselves and treated philosophy in their art. Plato is only a poet
writing in a loose, disconnected style. Timon calls him, as
an insult, a great forger of miracles.

Just as women use ivory teeth to replace their own that
are missing and, instead of their real complexion, make a
false one of foreign matter; as they pad their thighs with
cloth and felt, and their busts with cotton, and obviously
and to everyone's knowledge embellish themselves with a
false and borrowed beauty, so too does science (and even
our jurisprudence has, they say, legal fictions upon which it
founds the truth of its justice).

Our science offers us as an explanation, and as under-
lying principles of the universe, things that she herself in-
forms us were the product of human imagination. Those
epicycles, eccentrics, and concentrics which astrology uses to
explain the movement of its stars, it gives them to us as the
best it has been able to invent on this subject. Similarly,
moreover, philosophy presents to us not what is, or what it
believes, but the most pleasant and imposing of its inventions. Plato, speaking of his discussion of the state of our
body and that of beasts, declares: "That what we have said
is true, we should affirm it if we had on that point the con-

firmation of an oracle; we can only declare that it has the greatest appearance of truth of what we could say." . . .

I am grateful to the woman of Miletus who, seeing the philosopher Thales occupy himself continually in contemplation of the celestial vault and always keep his eyes turned heavenward, placed something in his way to make him stumble, in order to warn him that it would be time to amuse his thought with things that were in the clouds when he had taken care of those which were at his feet. She surely gave him good advice in advising him to look to himself rather than to heaven. For, as Cicero has Democritus say,

> What lies before his feet, no man regards;
> His eyes explore the vaulted arch of heaven.
> [Cicero, *De divinatione* II, 13]

But our condition makes the knowledge of what we have within our hands as remote from us, and as far above the clouds, as knowledge of the stars. As Socrates says in Plato, to whomever dabbles in philosophy one can reproach what that woman reproached Thales with, that he sees nothing of what is before him. For every philosopher is ignorant of what his neighbor does, yes, and of what he does himself, and of what they both are, whether beasts or men.

*Our own being is beyond
our understanding.*

Those people who consider Sebond's arguments too weak, who are ignorant of nothing, who govern the universe, who know everything,

> What causes rule the sea; what regulates the seasons;
> If stars move at their own free will or by command;
> What veils in darkness the moon's orb, and what reveals
>   it;
> What is the will and power in nature's complex plan
> Which joins in perfect harmony discordant things;
> [Horace, *Epistles* I, xii, 16]

have they not sometimes probed, amid their books, the difficulties which stand in the way of their knowing their own being? We see indeed that the finger moves and that the foot moves; that some parts move by themselves, without our leave, and that our will controls others; that a certain fear makes us flush, and a certain other turn pale; this notion affects our spleen only, and that one our brain; one makes us laugh, and another weep; a certain other chills us and paralyzes all our senses, and stops the movement of our limbs. At a certain sight, our stomach rises; at a certain other, some lower part. But how a spiritual impression produces such an effect in a massive and solid subject, and the nature of the linking and union of these admirable mechanisms, never has man known that. "All these things are impenetrable to human reason and hidden in the majesty of nature," says Pliny [*Natural History* II, 37]; and St. Augustine declares: "The manner in which the spirit is united with the body is completely marvelous, nor can it be understood by man; yet that union is man himself." [*City of God* XXXI, x] Such considerations, however, do not arouse men's doubts, for their opinions are received according to ancient beliefs, with authority and credit, as if they were religion and law. One accepts, as by rote, what is commonly held; one accepts this truth with all its structure and appendages of arguments and proofs, as a firm and solid whole which one no longer shakes, which one no longer judges. On the contrary, each vies with the others in plastering and fortifying this accepted belief with all that his reason can add— and the reason is an adaptable instrument, which can be made to serve any form. Thus the world is full of, and steeped in, inanities and falsehood.

The most logically constructed systems
are based on uncertain principles.

The reason that people rarely doubt things is that they never test common ideas; they don't probe their foundations, where the fault and weakness lie; they debate only about subordinate matters; they don't ask if that is true, but if it was understood in this way or in that. They don't ask if Galen said anything worthwhile, but if this is what he said, or something else. Really it was right that this check-rein on the liberty of our judgments, and this tyranny over our beliefs, should extend to the schools and the arts. The god of scholastic learning is Aristotle; it is sacrilegious to debate his laws as it was those of Lycurgus at Sparta. His doctrine serves as magisterial law, though it may by chance be as false as any other. I don't know why I shouldn't accept as readily either the ideas of Plato, or the Atoms of Epicurus, or the Plenum and the Void of Leucippus and Democritus, or the Water of Thales, or the Infinity of Nature of Anaximander, or the Air of Diogenes, or the Numbers and Symmetry of Pythagoras, or the Infinite of Parmenides, or the One of Musaeus, or the Water and Fire of Apollodorus, or the Similar Parts of Anaxagoras, or the Discord and Harmony of Empedocles, or the Fire of Heraclitus, or any other opinion of that infinite confusion of ideas and maxims which this fine human reason produces by its certitude and clearsightedness in everything it dabbles in, as I should accept the opinion of Aristotle, on this subject of the principles of natural things. He builds these principles out of three elements: matter, form, and privation. And what is more vain than to make emptiness itself a cause of the production of things? Privation is a negative; by what strange whim could he have made it the cause and origin of things which are? No one would dare disturb that belief, however, except as an exercise in logic. One debates nothing in Aristotle's teaching in order to put it in doubt, but only to defend the creator of the school against objections from outside: his authority is the limit beyond which it is not permitted to push any inquiry.

It is very easy, on accepted premises, to build anything you like, for, according to the principle and organization of this beginning, the rest of the pieces of the structure are easily put in place without any contradiction among them. By following this route, we find our argument well founded, and our reasoning rolls along easily, for our masters seize and occupy in our minds in advance as much ground as they need to conclude afterwards what they will, in the manner of geometricians, with their concessions demanded beforehand, the consent and approval which we accord them permitting them to lead us to left or right, and to spin us about at will. Whoever is believed in his presuppositions is our master and our god; he will take for his foundations a base so broad and so easy that, upon them, there will be no limit to the structure up which he can take us. In this practice and manner of conducting learning, we have taken at face value the statement by Pyathagoras that each expert must be believed in his field. The logician refers to the grammarian on the meaning of words; the rhetorician borrows from the logician the structure of his arguments; the poet borrows rhythms from the musician; the geometrician borrows proportions from the arithmetician; the metaphysicians take as a foundation the conjectures of physics. For each field of learning has its presupposed principles by means of which human judgment is held in check from all sides. If you happen to strike against this barrier in which lies the principal error, they straightway declare that there is no arguing with those who deny the principles.

Now there can be no universally valid principles for men unless the divinity has revealed them to them; all the rest, the beginning, the middle, and the end, is only dream and smoke. Against those who argue by presupposition, you must, contrary to all reason, presuppose the very axiom which is the subject of debate. For any human presupposition and any declaration has as much authority as any other, unless the reason establishes a difference. Thus one must weigh them all, and first of all the general ones and those which exercise a tyranny over us. . . .

[Philosophers] must not say to me: "It is true, for you see it and feel it thus"; they must tell me whether what I think I feel, I feel it therefore in reality; and if I do feel it, they must tell me afterwards why I feel it, and how, and what it is. They must tell me the name, the origin, the limits and the extent of heat, of cold; the nature of him who acts and him who undergoes; or they must abandon their profession, which is never to receive or approve anything except through the avenue of reason. Reason is their touchstone for all sorts of tests, but certainly it is a touchstone full of falsity, error, weakness, and incapacity. . . .

In the reproaches which philosophers address to one another over the dissensions of their opinions, an infinite number of such examples are to be found—not of arguments which are merely false, but arguments which are inept, inconsistent, and which convict their authors not so much of ignorance as of imprudence. Whoever would put together a sufficiently large collection of the stupid productions of human wisdom would reveal some marvelous things. I gladly assemble some as an exhibit, from a certain point of view no less useful to consider than sound and moderate opinions would be.

Let us judge in this way what we must think of man, his sense, and his reason, since in these great personages, who have carried human abilities so far, there are such obvious and such gross blunders. I prefer to believe that they have treated learning casually, as a plaything anyone can handle, and have sought amusement from reason as from a vain and frivolous instrument, setting forth all kinds of inventions and fancies, sometimes with more serious effort, sometimes with less. This same Plato who defined man as a chicken said elsewhere, following Socrates, that he does not know in truth what a man is, and that he is one of the elements of creation most difficult to know. By this variety and instability of opinions, they lead us as by the hand, tacitly, to this solution of their irresolution. They profess not to present always openly and in an obvious way what they think; they have hidden it sometimes beneath the fabulous shadows of poetry, and sometimes under some other disguise. As a consequence of our imperfection, raw meat is not always right for our stomach; we must dry it, modify it, and corrupt it. They do the same; they obscure sometimes their true opinions and judgments, and falsify them, in order to conform to public usage. They do not wish expressly to admit the ignorance and weakness of the human reason in order not to frighten children; but they reveal it to us sufficiently under the aspect of a confused and uncertain science.

In Italy I advised someone who had difficulty speaking Italian that, so long as he was seeking merely to make himself understood, without wishing to excel more brilliantly in it, he just employ the first words which came into his head, Latin, French, Spanish, or Gascon, and that by adding to them the Italian ending he would never fail to hit upon some dialect of the country, either Tuscan, or Roman, or Venetian, or Piedmontese, or Neapolitan, and to coincide with one of so many forms. In my opinion the same applies to philosophy; it has so many faces and so much variety, and has said so many things, that all our dreams and reveries have a place in it. Human fancy has never been able to imagine anything, for good or evil, which is not there. "Nothing so absurd can be said that it has not been said by some one of the philosophers." [Cicero, *De divinatione* II, 58] And in consequence I write more freely, according to my whims; the more so since I know that even though my ideas are born within me and follow no model, people will find them related to some old idea, and someone is sure to say: "That's where he got it!" . . .

The only certain truth
is revealed by God.

All things produced by our own reasoning and powers, whether true or false, are subject to doubt and debate. It is for the punishment of our pride and the instruction of our wretchedness and incapacity that God brought about the trouble and confusion of the old tower of Babel. All that we undertake without his assistance, all that we see without the lamp of his grace, is only vanity and folly; the very essence of truth, which is uniform and constant, we corrupt it and bastardize it by our weakness when fortune puts it in our hands. However man may seek his way by himself, God permits that he always reach this same confusion, of which he offers us such a vivid image by the just punishment with which he crushed the presumption of Nimrod and toppled the vain undertaking of the building of his pyramid: "I will destroy the wisdom of the wise, and will bring to nothing the understanding of the prudent." [I *Corinthians* I, 19] The diversity of languages and tongues with which he troubled that work, what else is it but that infinite and perpetual altercation and discordance of opinions and reasonings which accompany and confuse the vain structure of human learning? And confuse it to a useful purpose. What would restrain us, if we had a grain of knowledge? The saint pleased me greatly who declared, "The very obscurity concerning what is useful exercises humility or wears down pride." [St. Augustine, *City of God* XI, 22] To what point of presumption and insolence do we not carry our blindness and our stupidity?

But to come back to my subject, it was really right that we should be beholden to God alone, and to the goodness of his grace, for the truth of so noble a belief, since by his liberality alone we receive the fruit of immortality, which consists in the enjoyment of eternal bliss.

Let us confess ingenuously that we acquire truth through God alone, and by faith, for it is not learned from nature and by our reason. And he who probes his being and his powers, within and without, without this divine privilege, he who sees man without flattering him, will see in him neither efficacity nor faculty which can perceive anything other than death and the earth. The more we give, and owe, and restore to God, the more Christian is our attitude. . . .

Really Protagoras was telling us a pretty tall story when he made man the measure of all things, man who never even knew his own measure. If it is not he, his dignity will not admit that another creature should have that advantage. Now since he is himself so contrary, and since one judgment of his constantly invalidates another, that favorable proposition was only a mockery which led us to conclude by necessity the vanity of the measuring stick and of the measurer.

When Thales considers the knowledge of man very difficult for man, he lets him know that knowledge of anything else is impossible for him.

Montaigne warns against using the attack on reason he has just outlined.

You, for whom I have taken the trouble to expand so long a development more than is my wont, do not hesitate at all to defend Sebond by the ordinary form of debate in which you are every day instructed, and you will exercise in so doing your mind and your ingenuity. This last fencing trick must be used only as a final resort. It is a thrust of desperation, for which you must abandon your own weapons in order to make your opponent lose his, and a secret trick which must be used rarely and with caution. It is a very bold stroke to ruin yourself in order to ruin another.

One must not seek to die in order to avenge oneself, as Gobrias did. As he was locked in hand to hand battle with a lord of Persia, Darius came up with sword in hand, but he was afraid to strike for fear of smiting Gobrias; the latter cried out to him to strike boldly, even though he were to cut through both of them.

Arms and conditions of combat so desperate that it is beyond belief that either party should escape, these I have seen condemned when men have had recourse to them. The Portuguese captured fourteen Turks in the Indian Ocean who, impatient at their captivity, resolved and successfully undertook to reduce themselves, their masters, and the vessel to ashes by rubbing together nails from the ship until a spark fell on the kegs of gunpowder which were there.

Here we are coming up against the limits and remotest barriers of knowledge, in which extremes are vicious as they are in conduct. Keep to the middle road; it is not at all good to be so subtle and so clever. Remember what the Tuscan proverb says: "Who grows too sharp, cuts himself." [Petrarch, *Canzoniere* XXII, 48] I advise you, in your opinions and reasonings, as in your mode of living and everything else, moderation and temperance, and the avoidance of novelty and strangeness. All out of the ordinary ways annoy me. You who, by the authority which your high station lends you, and still more by the advantages which your personal qualities give you, are in a position to command whom you please, you ought to have turned over this task to someone who had made of letters his profession, and who would have aided you much better, and provided something richer than my fancies. However, this suffices for the use to which you are to put it.

CHAPTER IV

The Unreliability of the Senses

[*Summary*—Montaigne points out that both truth and error enter our consciousness through the channel of the senses, and that we are powerless to distinguish between them. Our perceptions vary with our state of health, our moods, our age. They are not uniform and cannot furnish a source of certain knowledge. Prejudices of all sorts affect our judgments. Montaigne—a former magistrate himself—cites the example of the judge whose findings are necessarily determined in part by personal considerations having nothing to do with an absolute and unattainable "justice." Since he recognizes how slight are the influences which shape our opinions, Montaigne considers it wise to retain the fundamental beliefs of the religion in which he was reared. He develops the notion of the relativity of justice and truth. Like everything in nature, beliefs, judgments, and opinions go through cycles of birth, development, and decay. While philosophers claim there are certain universal natural laws governing man, they are far from being in accord about them. All knowledge comes through our senses, and the senses are, as experience shows, completely unreliable. Animals doubtless possess senses we do not have, and for this reason our notion of the nature of things is incomplete. Montaigne cites numerous examples of the error and uncertainty of the operation of the senses. He further shows that our judgment is modified by attending sensual stimuli; our senses deceive our understanding. Indeed, life is, as it were, a kind of dream. Then he presents the modifications of our sense perceptions. Our senses grasp only their own feelings, and not the true essence of exterior things. Nothing remains unchanged in the flux of nature—neither our perceptions nor the objects we perceive. Essences cannot, then, be grasped, for they are changing constantly. God alone *is*, in a true sense; all else is in evolution. Only through his grace can we attain any real knowledge.]

71

*The mind must be subject
to strict controls.*

Epicurus said of the laws that the worst were so necessary to us that, without them, men would eat one another.
And Plato says approximately the same thing, that without
laws we should live as wild beasts, and he strives to prove it.

Our mind is a vagabond, dangerous, and rash instrument; it is difficult to combine order and restraint with it.
And, in my day, those who have some rare excellence above
others and some extraordinary keenness of intellect, we see
them almost all given to free thought and moral license. It
is a miracle if one encounters a single one whose behavior
is staid and sociable. It is proper to impose upon the human
spirit the most restrictive barriers possible. In study as in all
the rest one must count and control its steps, one must set
for it by rule the limits in which it is free to carry on its
explorations. One checks and binds it with religions, with
laws, with customs, with science, with precepts, with mortal
and immortal penalties and rewards; even so, one sees that
by its volatility and subtlety it escapes all these bonds. It is
an intangible thing which one cannot seize or strike, an
ever-changing and shapeless thing which cannot be bound
or held. Certainly there are few souls so well ordered, so
strong, and so noble that one can entrust to them their own
conduct, and which can, with moderation and without temerity, move freely, left to the liberty of their own judgments,
beyond the limits of common opinions. It is more expedient
to keep a watch over them. The mind is a dangerous sword,
even to its owner, unless he knows how to arm himself with
it in an orderly and discreet manner. And there is no animal
who more properly should wear blinders to keep his eyes in
due control straight before him, and to keep him from
wandering to this side or that, outside the path that custom
and laws trace for him. For this reason it will be better for
you to restrict yourself within the limits of accustomed
manners, whatever they may be, than to take flight into that

unbridled license. But if some one of these new scholars undertakes to display his cleverness in your presence, at the risk of his own salvation and of yours, to rid yourself of this dangerous infection which spreads every day in your courts, this antidote, in case of extreme need, will prevent the contagion of this venom hurting you or those about you. . . .

Theophrastus said that human knowledge, gathered through the senses, could judge the causes of things up to a certain point, but that having reached the most remote, the original causes, it had to stop and it was blunted either because of its own weakness or of the difficulty confronting it. That is a moderate and mild opinion, that our ability can lead us to the knowledge of some things, and that it has certain limits of capability beyond which it is rash to push it. This opinion is plausible, and advanced by conciliatory men; but it is difficult to give limits to our mind—it is curious and avid, and more likely to stop at a thousand paces than at fifty. Having proved by experience that where one had failed another succeeded, and that what was unknown to one century, the next one threw light upon; that the sciences and arts are not cast in a mold, but are formed and shaped little by little by handling and polishing them repeatedly as bears fashion their young by licking them at leisure—when, then, I lack the power to penetrate something, I do not stop probing and testing it; and by handling and kneading this new matter over again, stirring it and warming it up, I open up to him who follows me some facility to enjoy it more at ease, and make it for him more pliable and easier to handle,

> As beeswax softens in the sun's warm rays,
> And molded with the thumb takes many forms,
> And through being used becomes more useful still.
> [Ovid, *Metamorphoses* X, 284]

So too will the second open the way to the third, and that is why the difficulty must not make me despair, nor my failure either, for they are only mine. Man is as capable of all things as of a few. Now, if he admits, as Theophrastus says, the ignorance of first causes and principles, I declare that he should boldly abandon all the rest of his learning: if the foundation is lacking, all his reasoning crumbles; argumentation and research have no other goal and stopping point than principles. If this is not the end of his endeavors, he rushes into an infinite irresolution. "One thing cannot be more or less understood than another, for there is for all things only one way to understand them." [Cicero, *Academica* II, 51]

Now it is probable that, if the soul knew something, it would know itself; and if it knew something outside itself, it would be its body and envelope, before anything else. If one sees even today the gods of medicine quarrel with one another over our anatomy,

> Against Troy Vulcan took his stand,
> While on Troy's side Apollo stood;
> [Ovid, *Tristia* I, ii, 5]

when can we expect to see them in agreement? . . . If man does not know himself, how can he know his functions and his powers? Now I do not say that real knowledge may not happen to dwell within us, but it is by chance. And inasmuch as by the same path, in the same way, and through the same channels errors are received in our soul, it has no way of distinguishing them nor of separating truth from falsehood.

The followers of the Academy recognized some inclination of judgment, and thought it too rash to say that it wasn't more likely that snow was white than black, and that we were not more certain of the movement of a stone which leaves our hand than of the movement of the eighth sphere. And to avoid this difficult and strange notion, which indeed it is hard for us to conceive, although they establish that we are in no way capable of knowing, and that truth is buried in profound abysses where the human eye cannot penetrate, yet they admit some things as more probable than others, and recognize in their judgment that faculty of being able to lean toward one appearance rather than another. They allowed their judgment this propensity, while forbidding it any complete decision.

The opinion of the Pyrrhonians is bolder and, at the same time, it has a greater appearance of truth. For this Academic inclination and this leaning toward one proposition rather than another, what is it but the recognition of some more apparent truth in this one than in that one? If our understanding were capable of recognizing the form, the features, the bearing, and the countenance of truth, it would see truth entire as well as in part, nascent and imperfect. This appearance of verisimilitude which makes them incline to the left rather than to the right, magnify it; this ounce of verisimilitude which swings the balance, multiply it by a hundred, a thousand ounces; in the long run there will happen this, that the balance will swing completely in one direction and will record a definitive choice and a complete truth. But how do they let themselves yield to verisimilitude if they do not know the truth? How do they know the semblance of something whose essence they do not know? Either we can judge completely, or we are completely incapable of so doing. If our intellectual and perceptive faculties are without foundation and without footing, if they merely float and drift, in vain do we let our judgment be swayed by some part of their operation, whatever evidence it may seem to offer us; and the surest status for our understanding, and the happiest, would be for it to hold itself firm, erect, unbending, without movement and agitation. "Between true and false appearances, nothing determines the assent of the mind." [Cicero, *Academica* II, 28]

Many influences affect our
sensations and judgments.

That things are not in our minds in their form and essence, and do not enter there by their own force and authority, we see clearly enough. If that were so, we should therefore all receive them in the same way. Wine would be the same in the mouth of a sick person as in the mouth of one in good health. He whose fingers are chapped or numb would feel the same hardness in the wood or iron he handles as does another. Objects outside ourselves are placed, then, at our mercy; they enter our consciousness as we please. Now if on our side we received something without alteration, if the human grasp were sufficiently strong and firm to seize the truth by our own means, those means being common to all men, one man could pass that truth to another, from hand to hand. And at least there would be found in the world one thing, out of all those that are, which would be believed by men with a universal consent. But the fact that there is seen no proposition which is not debated or challenged among us, or which cannot be, shows well that our natural judgment does not seize very clearly what it grasps; for my judgment cannot make the judgment of my companion receive it, which is evidence that I seized it by some means other than a natural power which is in me and in all men.

Let us leave aside that infinite confusion of opinions which is seen among philosophers themselves, and that perpetual and universal debate about the knowledge of things. For we can accept as certain that on no subject are men (I mean the best endowed, the most able scholars) in agreement—they do not agree that the sky is above our heads, for those who doubt everything doubt that, too; and those who deny that we can understand anything say that we have not understood that the sky is above our heads; and these two opinions are, by weight of numbers, by far the strongest.

Apart from this infinite diversity and division, by the confusion which our judgment gives us and by the uncertainty which each feels in himself, it is easy to see that its stability is ill assured. How diversely do we judge things? How many times do we change our ideas? What I hold today and what I believe, I hold it and believe it with all my faith; all the instruments and mechanisms of my being grasp this opinion and guarantee it to me by all that is in their power. I cannot accept any truth or hold it with more strength than I do this one. I give myself over to it completely, in all sincerity; but has it not happened to me, not once, but a hundred, but a thousand times, and every day, to have embraced with all these same means, and with the same conviction, something else which I have since judged false? At least one must grow wise at one's own expense. If I have often found myself betrayed by such appearances, if my touchstone ordinarily proves false, and my balance uneven and inaccurate, what greater assurance can I have this time than before? Is it not stupid of me to let myself be duped so often by the same guide? However, if fortune makes us change position five hundred times, if unceasingly she keeps removing one opinion and replacing it by another in our belief as cargo is loaded and unloaded in a ship, always the present opinion, the latest one, is the certain and infallible one. For this opinion, one must abandon wealth, honor, life, and salvation, and everything:

> A new discovery o'ershadows all which came before,
> And changes the esteem we held them in.
> [Lucretius V, 1414]

Whatever they may preach to us, whatever we may learn, we must always remember that it is a man who gives and receives; it is a mortal hand which presents it; it is a mortal hand which accepts it. The things which come to us from heaven have alone the right and authority to arouse conviction; they alone bear the mark of truth, which also we do not see with our eyes, nor do we receive it by our means. That holy and mighty image could not reside in such a mean abode, unless God for that service prepared it, unless God reshaped it and strengthened it by his grace and special and supernatural favor.

At least our faulty condition ought to make us behave with greater moderation and reserve in our changes. We ought to remember, whatever we may receive in our understanding, that we often accept false things, and that it is by these same instruments which often contradict themselves and are mistaken.

Now it is no marvel if they contradict themselves, being so easily bent and twisted by the slightest events. It is certain that our perception, our judgment, and the faculties of our soul in general suffer according to the movements and alterations of the body, which alterations are continual. Is our mind not more alert, our memory more prompt, our reasoning more keen in health than in illness? Do not joy and gaiety make us perceive the subjects which are presented to our senses under quite a different appearance than do grief and melancholy? Do you think that the verses of Catullus or of Sappho give pleasure to a greedy and grumpy old man as they do to a young man, vigorous and spirited? When Cleomenes, the son of Anaxandridas, was ill, his friends reproached him that he had new and unaccustomed moods and fancies. "I should think so," he said, "for I am not the same person I was when I was well; since I am different, my opinions and fancies are different, too." In the legal fraternity of our lawcourts there is a remark frequently applied to criminals who find the judges in a good humor, gentle and mild: *Gaudeat de bona fortuna*—Let him rejoice in this good fortune. For it is certain that by chance judgments are sometimes more inclined toward condemnation, are more bristling and harsh, and at other times gentler, more tolerant, and more inclined toward pardon. If a judge brings with him from his home the pain of gout, jealousy, or anger at a theft made by his servant, having his whole nature colored by wrath and steeped in it, there can be no doubt that his judgment will be affected by it and inclined toward harshness. The venerable senate of the Areopagus sat at night lest the sight of those appearing before it might corrupt its justice. The very air and the serenity of the sky bring about some change in us, as is stated in these verses from the Greek in Cicero,

> The minds of men are changed as father Jupiter
> Sends down upon the earth the sun's productive rays.
> [adapted from the *Odyssey* XVIII, 135]

It is not merely fever, drink, and great accidents which upset our judgment; the slightest things in the world overturn it. We must not doubt, though we do not realize it, that if a continuous fever can overwhelm our spirit, so a tertian fever brings to it some alteration according to its measure and proportion. If apoplexy dulls and extinguishes completely the clarity of our intelligence, one must not doubt that a common cold disturbs it. Consequently scarcely is it possible to find a single hour in life when our judgment is quite undisturbed, our body being subject to so many continual changes, and controlled by so many organs that (as physicians tell me) it is most unlikely that there should not always be some one of them not functioning in unison with the others.

*Our reason a variable and
untrustworthy instrument.*

Moreover, such illness is not discovered readily, unless it is quite extreme and beyond remedy, the more so since the reason always carries on, in a staggering, limping, and disjointed fashion, dealing similarly with falsehood and with truth. It it thus difficult to discover its error and its improper functioning. I still call "reason" that appearance of rationalizing that each creates within himself—that reason, of such a condition that there can be a hundred contrary ones about a single subject, is an instrument of lead and wax, which can be stretched, bent, and accommodated to all biases and all measures; all that is lacking is the capacity to know how to control it. No matter how good a judge's intention, if he does not observe himself closely (and few people bother to do that) the prejudice of friendship, family ties, beauty, and vengeance, and not even things so weighty, but that fortuitous instinct which makes us favor one thing more than another, and which determines, without the approval of our reason, our choice between two similar objects, or some slight influence of similar insignificance, can insinuate in our judgment a favorable or unfavorable attitude toward a case and cause the balance to swing in a certain direction.

I who watch myself closely, who never cease my constant self-scrutiny like one who hasn't much to do elsewhere,

> Quite unconcerned about what king is feared
> In frozen lands beneath the Arctic Bear,
> Or what makes Tiridates tremble
> [Horace, *Carmina* 1, xxvi, 3]

scarcely dare I say the vanity and weakness which I find in myself. My foot is so uncertain and my step so unsure, I find myself so prone to stumble and so ready to fall, and my vision is so disturbed, that when I have not eaten I feel quite another person than after a meal; if my health is favorable and the weather fine, then at once I am a good fellow; if I have a corn pressing on my toe, then I am gloomy, disagreeable, and unapproachable. The same gait of a horse seems to me at one moment rough and at another easy, and the same road sometimes shorter, sometimes longer, and the same form now more and now less attractive. Now I bustle about doing everything, now I do nothing; what is a pleasure for me at this moment will be sometimes a burden. There rise within me a thousand indiscreet and casual agitations. Either the melancholy humor governs me, or the choleric; and by its own authority, at one moment grief prevails in me, and at another joy. When I pick up books, I may note in a certain passage excellent beauty of content and style which impresses my mind; when another time I return to the same passage, it does me no good to turn it and to view it from all angles, it does me no good to squeeze it and manipulate it; it is for me an unfamiliar and formless mass.

In my own writings, I don't always find again the tone

of my original idea. I don't know what I intended to say, and I often torment myself to correct my writings and to put into them a new meaning because I have lost the first one, which was better. I go constantly to and fro; my judgment does not always pull straight ahead; it floats aimlessly, it drifts,

> Like a frail bark caught by a furious storm
> Upon the sea's immensity.
>   [Catullus XXV, 12]

Many a time (as I am wont to do quite readily) having undertaken as an exercise and amusement to support an opinion contrary to my own, my mind, applying itself and evolving in that direction, inclines me so completely toward that opinion that I can no longer find the justification for my earlier belief, and I abandon it. I tend to fall in whatever direction I chance to lean, and I am carried along with all my weight.

*Influence of emotion
on judgment.*

Each would say approximately the same thing about himself, if he examined himself as I do. Preachers know that the emotion which comes over them as they speak animates them toward belief, and that in anger we apply ourselves more to the defense of our proposition, take it into our being, and embrace it with more vigor and approval than we do when our emotions are cool and calm. You merely relate a case to a lawyer, and he answers you hesitatingly and without assurance; you feel that it is a matter of indifference for him to undertake to support one side or the other. If you have paid him well to sink his teeth into the problem and to examine it thoroughly, if he begins to take an interest in it, then his will is stirred concerning it. His reason and his knowledge are aroused at the same time; there is an obvious and indubitable truth which is presented to his understanding; he discovers in it a quite new light,

and believes so sincerely, and convinces himself of it. Indeed, I do not know whether the ardor which is born of
vexation and stubbornness in facing the imposing power and
violence of authority and of danger, or the interest of his
reputation, has not persuaded many a man to support, even
at the risk of his life, an opinion for which among his
friends and at liberty, he would not have been willing to lift
a finger.

The shocks and agitations which our soul receives
through bodily passions can have a strong influence upon it,
but even more is it moved by its own passions, which affect
it so strongly that it can perhaps be maintained that it has
no other motion and movement than determined by its winds
and that, without their propulsion, it would remain inactive,
like a ship on the open sea, which the winds no longer
assist. And were one to maintain this notion, following the
school of the Peripatetics, he would not be wronging us
greatly, since it is known that most of the noblest actions of
the soul stem from and have need of that drive of the passions. Valor, they say, cannot reach its greatest heights
without the assistance of anger. "Always was Ajax brave,
but bravest, however, in his madness." [Cicero, *Tusculan
Disputations* IV, 23] Nor does one pursue the wicked or
one's enemies with sufficient vigor unless one is filled with
anger. And they wish the lawyer to inspire the judges with
wrath in order to obtain justice from them. Strong passions
stirred Themistocles and stirred Demosthenes; they spurred
philosophers to efforts, vigils, and wanderings; they lead us
to honor, learning, and health, which are useful ends. And
that cowardice of the soul in suffering boredom and annoy-
ance serves to nourish in the conscience penitence and re-
morse, and to make us feel for our punishment the scourges
of God and the rigors of civil correction. Compassion serves
as a goad to clemency, and the prudence to preserve and
control ourselves is aroused by our fear. And how many fine
actions are prompted by ambition? How many by pride? No
eminent and strong virtue, in short, is without some dis-

ordered agitation. Would that be one of the reasons which might have prompted the Epicureans to free God from any care and solicitude for our affairs, the more so since the very effects of his goodness could not be directed toward us without disturbing his peace through passions, which are like stings and promptings driving the soul to virtuous actions? Or else did they believe otherwise and consider the passions as tempests which shamefully debauch the soul in its tranquility? "As we call the calm of the sea the absence over its waves of even the slightest breath, so it may be affirmed that peace and tranquility of the soul is the state in which no passion can disturb it." [Cicero, *Tusculan Disputations* V, 6]

What differences of sense and reason, what contrast of imaginations, the diversity of our passions offers us! What assurance can we then draw from a thing so instable and so fluid, subject by its condition to be dominated by confusion, never proceeding except by a forced and unnatural gait? If our judgment is governed by disease itself and by passions, if it is from folly and temerity that it is obliged to receive its impressions of things, what certainty can we expect from it?

Is it not rash on the part of philosophy to consider that men produce their greatest effects—those closest to the divine—when they are beside themselves, and furious, and mad? We improve ourselves by depriving ourselves of our reason and putting it to sleep? The two natural ways to enter the private chambers of the gods and to foresee there the course of destinies are madness and sleep. This is amusing to consider: by the disorder which the passions bring to our reason, we become virtuous; by the utter destruction of reason, which madness or the semblance of death bring, we become prophets and seers. Never more readily did I believe anything concerning our reason. This is a pure transport inspired in the philosophic mind by holy truth which wrests from it, contrary to the philosophers' intention, the admission that the tranquil state of our soul, the calm state, the most healthy state which philosophy can acquire, is not its best state. Our waking life is more asleep than is sleep; our wisdom is less wise than our folly; our dreams are better than our reasonings; the worst refuge which we can seek is within ourselves. But does philosophy not realize that we are alert enough to note that that voice which makes the spirit so clear-sighted, so great, so perfect when it is outside man, and so terrestrial, ignorant, and blind when it is in man, is a voice arising from the spirit which is a part of that same man, terrestrial, ignorant, and blind, and for that reason a voice neither to be trusted nor believed?

Out of the recognition of his changeable
nature, Montaigne has drawn a
certain constancy of beliefs.

Being of a mild and dull disposition, I do not have much experience with those vehement agitations, most of which suddenly take our soul by surprise, without giving it leisure to gather its wits. But that passion that they say is produced by idleness in the heart of young men, although it develops with leisure and a measured progress, reveals quite obviously, to those who have tried to oppose its efforts, the force of that change and alteration which our judgment suffers. In other days I undertook to hold myself tense in order to meet and resist it (for so far am I from being one of those who invite vices, that I do not even follow them unless they sweep me along); I felt it awakening, growing, and increasing in spite of my resistance, and finally, like a seeing and living being, seize me and take possession of me in such a way that, as in a drunkenness, the images of things began to appear to me other than they usually did. I saw the charms of the object of my constant desires obviously growing and increasing, and magnified and swollen by the breath of my imagination. I saw the difficulties of my undertaking eased and evened out; my reason and my conscience seemed to withdraw into the background. But, this fire having burned itself out, all of a sudden I saw, as in a flash of lightning, my soul regain another sort of view, another state, and another judgment. I saw the difficulties of retreat seem to me great and invincible, and the same things of a quite different taste and appearance than the warmth of desire had made me find in them. Which was the truer impression? Pyrrho doesn't know at all. We are never without illness. Fevers have their heat and their cold; from the effects of a burning passion we fall back into the effects of a chilling passion.

As far as I had rushed forward, just so far do I hasten back:

> As when the sea, rushing with rhythmic swirl of waves,
> Now pours ashore to hurl its breakers on the rocks,
> And, foaming, floods in its embrace the farthest sands;
> And now speeds backwards as it sucks the rolling stones,
> And with receding waters withdraws again from shore.
> [Virgil, *Aeneid* XI, 624]

Now out of the knowledge of this changeable nature of mine, I have by chance engendered within myself some constancy of opinions, and I have scarcely altered my early and natural ones. For, whatever plausibility there may be in new ideas, I do not change readily lest I have occasion to lose in so doing. And, since I am not capable of choosing, I take the choice of others and remain in the position where God placed me. Otherwise, I could not keep myself from rolling constantly. So, by God's grace, I have kept completely, without agitation and disturbance of my conscience, the old beliefs of our religion, in spite of all the sects and divisions which our century has produced. The writings of the ancients (I mean the good writings, substantial and solid) attract me and stir me almost as they wish; the one I am listening to seems to me always the strongest; I find that each in turn is right, even though they contradict one another. One must recognize that facility which great minds have to make whatever they wish seem plausible, and the fact that there is nothing so strange but they undertake to color it sufficiently to fool a simple nature such as mine; that shows obviously the weakness of their proof. The sky

and the stars revolved for three thousand years; everyone
had believed so until Cleanthes of Samos or, according to
Theophrastus, Nicetas of Syracuse took it into his head to
maintain that it was the earth which moved around the
oblique circle of the Zodiac, spinning on its axis; and, in our
day, Copernicus has so well established that doctrine that he
uses it in a quite systematic way for all astronomical compu-
tations. What shall we draw from that, if not that we
should not worry which of the two systems is true? And who
knows that a third opinion, a thousand years from now, may
not overthrow the two previous ones?

> So rolling time affects the status of all things:
> What once was held in high esteem, from honor falls;
> Now something new prevails, emerging out of scorn—
> Each day it's more desired, receives bouquets of praise,
> And among men it holds a place of highest honor.
> [Lucretius V, 1275]

Distrust of new doctrines.

Thus when we encounter some new doctrine, we have
good reason to distrust it, and to consider that before it was
produced its contrary was in vogue; and as that earlier doctrine was overthrown by this one, there can well be born in
the future a third discovery which will similarly upset the
second one. Before the principles which Aristotle introduced
were generally accepted, other principles satisfied the human
reason as his satisfy us now. What warrant do his have,
what special privilege, that the course of our seeking ends
with them, and that to them belongs for all time dominion
over our belief? They are no more exempt from being ousted
than were the ideas which preceded them. When a new
argument is urged upon me, it is up to me to consider that,
where I cannot find a satisfactory answer, someone else will;
for to believe all the appearances which we cannot explain
away is to be a great simpleton. Such willingness to believe

would lead the common throng of men (and we are all of the common throng) to have beliefs which spin about like a weathervane; for their soul, being soft and without resistance, would be forced to receive unceasingly new impressions one on top of the other, the latest always effacing the trace of the preceding one. He who feels weak must answer, as they do in the law courts, that he will seek advice on the matter, or rely upon those wiser men under whom he served his apprenticeship. How long has the art of medicine existed? They say that a newcomer, Paracelsus by name, is changing and overthrowing the whole order of ancient rules, and maintains that heretofore medicine has served only to kill men. I believe that he will easily verify that; but as for submitting my life to the test of his new experience, I think that would not be great wisdom.

One must not believe everyone, the saying goes, because everyone can say all manner of things. . . .

Influence of environment on attitudes and temperament.

If nature includes also within the course of its ordinary development, as it does all other things, men's beliefs, judgments, and opinions; if they have their cycle, their season, their birth, their death, as cabbages do; if heaven agitates them and sweeps them along in its usual way, what permanent authority to guide us can we attribute to them? If by experience we learn that the form of our being depends upon the air, the climate, and the soil where we are born, not merely our complexion, stature, temperament, and bearing, but also the faculties of the soul—"and the climate contributes not only to bodily strength, but likewise to intellectual powers," [Vegetius I, 2]—and if the goddess who founded the city of Athens chose for its site a climate which made men prudent, as the priests of Egypt taught Solon—"The air at Athens is rare, and as a consequence, then, the Athenians are considered more keen; the air at

Thebes is heavy, and therefore the Thebans are dull and coarse" [Cicero, *De fato,* IV]—just as fruits and animals are born different from one another, men are born also more or less pugnacious, just, temperate, and docile: here subject to drunkenness, elsewhere to thievery or lewdness; here inclined to superstition, and elsewhere to incredulity; in one place to liberty, and in another to servitude; capable of learning a science or art, dull-witted or ingenious, obedient or rebellious, good or evil, according to the influence of the place where they are put, and they acquire a different temperament if, like trees, they are transplanted. That is why Cyrus refused to allow the Persians to abandon their harsh and mountainous homeland to settle in a gentle and level region, saying that rich and soft soils make men soft, and fertile soils make minds unproductive. If we see sometimes one art or one opinion flourish, and sometimes another, through some influence of heaven; if we see a certain century produce certain natures and form men of a certain bent; if we see the minds of men sometimes vigorous and sometimes barren like our fields; what, then, becomes of all those fine prerogatives of mankind of which we are wont to boast? Since a wise man can be mistaken, and a hundred men, and many nations, indeed since the whole of mankind, as we see, can be mistaken for several centuries on this subject or that, what assurance have we that sometimes it ceases to be mistaken, and that in our own age it is not in error?

We do not know our own needs
nor our true good.

It seems to me, among other evidences of our weakness, that this one ought not to be forgotten: that even through desire man is unable to identify what he needs. Neither through enjoyment, nor through imagination and wishing, can we agree on what we need in order to be satisfied. Let us permit our thought complete freedom to cut its cloth and sew it as it will; even then it will not succeed in desiring what is suitable for it, and in satisfying itself.

some see it in learning, some in the absence of pain, some in not letting oneself be deceived by appearances, and to this last idea seems to be related the following one, of ancient Pythagoras,

> Let nothing rouse your wonder and desire, my friend
> For that is just about the only way for man
> To find and keep some share of happiness
> [Horace, *Epistles* I, vi, 1]

which is the goal of the Pyrrhonian sect. Aristotle attributes to greatness of soul the ability to marvel at nothing. And Arcesilas said that to hold the judgment in a rigid and inflexible state was good, whereas to yield and to choose were vices and evils. It is true that in so far as he set it up as a firm rule he was deviating from Pyrrhonism. The Pyrrhonians, when they say that the supreme good is *ataraxia,* which is suspension of the judgment, do not make of this a truly affirmative declaration; but the same sensitivity of their being which makes them avoid precipices and protect themselves from the chill air presents to them this idea and makes them refuse any other.

Justus Lipsius[7] is the most learned man left to us today, of a most cultivated and judicious mind, truly akin to my Turnebus; how I wish that while I live either he, or someone else, might resolve (and have the health and the leisure to carry it out) to collect in a compilation, according to their divisions and categories, sincerely and carefully, in so far as we can see them, the opinions of ancient philosophy on the subject of our being and our morals; I should want him to note the quarrels, reputation, and following of the various schools, and the fidelity of the authors and their disciples to their precepts in the memorable and exemplary events of their lives. What a beautiful and useful work that would be!

---

[7] Flemish scholar (1547-1606), best known for his edition of Tacitus.

*Relativity of virtue
and justice.*

Moreover, if it is from ourselves that we draw the
government of our lives, what confusion we are casting ourselves into! For the most acceptable advice our reason can
offer us is in general for each to obey the laws of his own
country. This is the opinion of Socrates, inspired, he declares, by divine counsel. And what does our reason mean
by this declaration except that the only principle governing
duty is a fortuitous one? The truth must be always and universally one. If man knew any virtue and justice which had
a real form and essence, he would not make them dependent
upon the set of customs of this country or of that; it would
not be from the peculiar notions of Persia or India that
virtue would derive its form. There is nothing subject to
more continual dispute than laws. During my lifetime I have
seen those of our English neighbors changed three or four
times, not only laws of a political nature (where one is willing not to demand constancy), but laws on the most important subject which can be, namely religion. I feel grief and
shame because of it, the more so since it is a nation with
which the people of my province used to have an especially
close connection so that there still remain in my family some
traces of our old kinship.

And in our own country, I have seen some things which
used to be for us capital crimes become legitimate; and we,
who hold other things as legitimate, run the risk, according
to the uncertainty of the fortunes of war, of being one day
guilty of high treason against both the King and God, our
justice falling under the mercy of injustice and, in the space
of a few years of subjection, assuming a contrary essence.

How could that god of antiquity more clearly mark in
human knowledge our total ignorance concerning the divine
being, and inform men that religion was only a product of
their imagination, useful as a unifying bond to their society,
than by declaring, as he did to those who inquired about it

before his tripod, that the true worship for each man was the one that he found observed by the custom of the place where he was? O God! what obligation do we not have to the goodness of our sovereign creator for having rid our belief of those stupid, vagabond, and arbitrary forms of worship, and for having established it upon the eternal foundation of his holy word!

What, then, will philosophy tell us in this need of ours? That we should follow the laws of our country, that is to say that billowing sea of opinions of a people or of a prince, which will paint justice for me with as many colors and will recast it into as many aspects as there will be changes of passion among them? I cannot have so flexible a judgment. What virtue is it which I saw yesterday esteemed, and which tomorrow will be so no more, and which becomes a crime as soon as one crosses a river?

What kind of truth is it for which these mountains mark the limit, and which is falsehood for those people who dwell on the other side?

So-called natural laws
lack universality.

But they are amusing when, to give some certitude to the laws, they say that there are some firm, perpetual, and immutable, which they call natural laws, which are imprinted in the human race by the nature of man's very essence. And of those laws, some consider there are three, some four, others more or fewer—an indication that they are of as doubtful a stamp as all the rest. Now the philosophers are so unfortunate (for how can I call that anything but misfortune, that out of so infinite a number of laws there does not happen to be at least one that the fickleness and changeability of fate has permitted to be universally accepted by the consent of all nations?) they are, I repeat, so luckless that of those three or four chosen laws there is not a single one which is not contradicted and disavowed, not by one nation, but by many. Now the universality of their acceptance is the only probable sign by which one can deduce the existence of any natural laws. For what nature would really have ordained for us, we should doubtless follow by common consent. And not only every nation, but every individual man, would recognize the force and violence exercised over him by anyone who should seem to make him go against that law. Let them show me, as an example, just one such law.

Protagoras and Aristo gave to the justice of the laws no other essence than the authority and opinion of the legislator; and, except for that, "good" and "honest" lost their meanings and remained vain names of indifferent things. Thrasymachus, in Plato's *Republic,* considers that there is no other right than the good pleasure of the stronger man. There is nothing in which the world offers greater variety than in customs and laws. A certain thing is here abominable which elsewhere brings commendation, as does in Lacedemonia the light-fingered skill of the thief. Marriages between close relatives are among our capital offenses; they are elsewhere held in honor:

> It is reported there are nations of the world
> Where mothers wed their sons, and fathers may be joined
> In marriage to their daughters, increasing doubly thus
> Filial affection by uniting it with love.
> [Ovid, *Metamorphoses* X, 331]

The murder of children, of parents, traffic in women, trade in stolen goods, freedom for every sort of sensual excess, there is, after all, nothing so extreme that it is not accepted by the custom of some nation.

It is believable that there are natural laws, as is seen among other creatures; but among us they are lost, for this fine human reason insinuates itself everywhere in order to dominate and command, befogging and confusing the appearance of things according to its vanity and inconstancy. "And so nothing is our own any more; what I call ours is a product of art." [Based on Cicero, *De finibus* V, 21]

*Diversity of viewpoints results in diversity
of judgments and customs.*

The same subjects may be viewed according to various lights and ways; that is the principal source of the diversity of opinions. One nation looks upon a subject according to one of its aspects, and stops there; another nation considers another aspect.

There is nothing so horrible to imagine as eating one's father. Peoples who in antiquity had that custom saw in it, however, a proof of loyalty and true affection, seeking in that way to give to their parents the most worthy and honorable sepulcher, making the bodies and remains of their fathers dwell within themselves and, as it were, in the very marrow of their bones, giving them a sort of life and regenerating them by transmutation into their living flesh by means of digestion and assimilation. It is easy to consider what cruelty and abomination it would have been, to men steeped in and imbued with this superstition, to cast the remains of parents into the corruption of the earth to become food for beasts and worms.

Lycurgus considered in theft the swiftness, dexterity, boldness, and skill necessary in surreptitiously taking something from one's neighbor, and the utility which the public derives from it, for each sees more carefully to the protection of what is his; and he concluded that from this double teaching, in attack and in defense, was to be drawn a profit for military discipline (which was the principal knowledge and strength which he wished to inculcate in the Spartans) —and this, he felt, was of greater consideration than the disorder and injustice involved in appropriating what belongs to others.

Dionysius the tyrant offered Plato a robe of Persian style, long, damasked, and perfumed; Plato refused it, saying that, being born a man, he would not willingly clothe himself in a woman's costume; but Aristippus accepted it, with the answer that no accouterment could corrupt a

chaste heart. His friends chided him for his cowardice in
taking so little to heart the fact that Dionysius had spit in
his face. Fishermen, he replied, endure being bathed in the
waves of the sea, from head to foot, in order to catch a
gudgeon. Diogenes was washing his cabbages, and seeing
Aristippus said to him: "If you knew how to live on cab-
bage, you wouldn't pay court to a tyrant." To this Aristippus answered: "If you knew how to live among men, you
wouldn't wash cabbages." That's how reason lends plausibility to various conclusions. It's a two-handled jar, which
one can seize with the right or the left hand:

> It's war you bring, o land which is to be our home;
> For war your horses are equipped; they threaten war.
> Yet these same horses oft are trained to wear the gear
> Of peaceful vehicles and join to bear the yoke
> Under a friendly rein. Hope there is for peace!
> [Virgil, *Aeneid* III, 539]

People urged Solon not to shed for the death of his
son useless and impotent tears. It is precisely for that reason,
he said, that I shed them with greater justification, since
they are indeed useless and impotent. Socrates' wife was
bemoaning her loss in this wise: "Oh, how unjustly those
wicked judges put him to death." "Would you prefer, then,
that it be deserved?" they answered her.

We have our ears pierced; the Greeks considered that
a mark of servitude. We hide in order to have intercourse
with our wives; the Indians do so in public. The Scythians
sacrificed foreigners in their temples; elsewhere temples
serve as a place of refuge.

> Thence stems the madness of the mass of men,
> For everywhere they hate their neighbor's gods,
> And hold that those alone to which they bow
> Are worthy of belief.
> [Juvenal XV, 37]

I have heard of a judge who, when he encountered a bitter conflict between Bartolus and Baldus,[8] and a case confused by many contradictions, would write in the margin of his book, "Find for the friend"; that is to say that the truth was so confused and debatable that in such an affair he could favor whichever party might seem good to him. It was only a matter of lack of wit and capacity which kept him from writing everywhere: "Find for the friend." Lawyers and judges of our day find in all cases a great enough number of angles to justify whatever decision may seem good to them. In such an infinitely varied field of knowledge, dependent on the authority of so many opinions and of such an arbitrary nature, there must necessarily arise an extreme confusion of judgments. And so there is scarcely any lawsuit so clear that there are not different views concerning it. What one court has judged, another court judges in quite the opposite way, and even the same court does so at another time. Of this we see constant examples in the freedom with which the decrees of our courts are disregarded, and people run from one judge to another to decide the same case. This is a noteworthy blemish upon the ceremonious authority and reputation of our justice. . . .

Laws receive their authority from practice and custom. It is dangerous to trace them back to their source; they swell and grow nobler as they roll along, like our rivers. Follow them upstream to their source, and it is only a trickle of water, scarcely recognizable, which grows thus in pride and strength as it flows along. Observe the original considerations which first set in motion this famous torrent, full of dignity, and inspiring awe and reverence; you will find them so slight and so tenuous that it is no wonder those people who weigh all things and subject them to reason, and accept nothing on authority and faith, are often in their judgments very far indeed from those of the public. . . .

---

[8] Famous Italian legal authorities of the 14th century.

*Conflicting interpretation
of events and of texts.*

Heraclitus and Protagoras, because wine seems bitter to
the sick man and pleasing to one in health, because the oar
seems bent in the water and straight to those who see it out
of the water, and because of such other contrary appearances which are found in things, argued that all things had
in themselves the causes of these appearances, and that there
was in the wine some bitterness transferred to the taste of
the invalid, and in the oar some nature of curvature made
perceptible to one who saw it in the water. And so on with
other things. Which is to say that everything is in all things,
and consequently nothing in any, for nothing is where everything is.

This opinion puts me in mind of the experience we
have that there is no meaning or appearance, either straight,
or bitter, or sweet, or curved, that the human mind does
not find in the writings which it undertakes to examine. And
out of the clearest, purest, most perfect utterance which is
possible, how much falseness and lying has not been drawn?
What heresy has not found in it sufficient basis and testimony to proclaim and defend itself? It is for that reason
that the authors of such errors are never willing to deviate
from this sole proof—the testimony of the interpretation of
words. A person of dignity, wishing to make me approve
on good authority the search for the philosopher's stone to
which he has devoted himself completely, offered me recently
in support of his claim five or six passages of the Bible in
which he said he had at the outset found justification in
order to keep his conscience clear (for he is of the eccle-
siastical calling); and, in truth, his discovery of these texts
was not only amusing, but even well calculated to serve as a
defense of that fine science.

It is in this way that prophecies come to be believed.
There is no prophet, if he has sufficient prestige that people
will bother to thumb through his writings, and seek care-

fully all the hidden recesses and reflections of his words, whom you cannot make say anything you wish, as was the case with the Sibyls; for there are so many manners of interpretation that it is difficult for an ingenious mind, by an oblique or direct interpretation, not to find on any subject something which seems plausibly to serve its purpose.

That is why a cloudy and ambiguous style is in such frequent and traditional use! Let the author thus succeed in attracting and absorbing posterity (an end which not only ability can attain, but, equally well or better, the chance popularity of the subject); moreover, let him express himself, out of stupidity or by cleverness, in a somewhat obscure and contradictory way—it matters not a whit to him! Many minds, shaking and sifting his writings, will extract from them a quantity of ideas either in accordance with his own, or on a tangent, or quite opposed to them, and all these ideas will redound to his honor. He will see himself enriched by the gifts of his disciples, like schoolmasters during the Lendit fair.[9]

That is what has caused the success of many worthless things, what has given many writings a reputation, and filled them with whatever matter one wished—a single one receiving thousands and thousands of values, and as many various images and ideas as we please. Is it possible that Homer meant all that interpreters make him say? Is it possible that he intended such numerous and varied interpretations that theologians, legislators, captains, philosophers, and all sorts of people who treat learned subjects, however differently and conflictingly they treat them, should base themselves on him, should refer to him, should make of him the general master for all functions, works, and trades, and the general counselor for all undertakings? Whoever has had need of oracles and predictions has found them for his

---

[9] An important academic festival in June; supplies of parchment were purchased at the Lendit Fair, and students paid their tuition fees to their professors.

purpose in Homer's works. It is remarkable how a learned person, a friend of mine, draws from them in support of our religion so many and such admirable passages! And one cannot easily convince him that such is not Homer's intention (and Homer is as familiar to him as to any man of our day). And what he finds in support of ours, many in antiquity had found in support of their religions.

Just see how Plato is tormented and disturbed! Each one, for his own reputation, seeks to find support in his works, and puts him on the side he wishes. Plato is paraded out, and inserted into all the new opinions people receive; and they even set him against himself according to the new directions that thought takes. They make him disavow in their judgment the legitimate customs of his day, the more so because they are not legitimate in ours.

All that is done with a keenness and force in proportion to the interpreter's forcefulness and keenness of mind.

Upon the same foundation which Heraclitus had, and from which he drew his dictum that all things had in them the qualities which one found in them, Democritus drew a quite contrary conclusion, namely that objects did not possess at all what we found in them; and from the fact that honey was sweet to one and bitter to another, he concluded that it was neither sweet nor bitter. The Pyrrhonians would say that they know not whether it is sweet or bitter, or neither one nor the other, or both, for they reach always the highest point of doubt.

The disciples of Aristippus of Cyrene held that nothing was perceptible from the outside, and that only what touched us inwardly was perceptible, such as pain and pleasure, not recognizing either tone or color, but only certain sensations which came to us from them, and teaching that man had no other foundation for his judgment. Protagoras considered that the truth for any person is the way things seem to him. The Epicureans place every judgment in the senses, both in regard to the knowledge of things and in regard to pleasure.

Plato wished that the judgment of truth, and truth itself, be completely separated from opinions and from the senses, and that they should belong to the mind and to cogitation.

The source of all our "knowledge"
is in the senses.

This subject has brought me to the consideration of the senses, and therein lie the greatest source and proof of our ignorance. Everything that is known is doubtless known through the faculties of the knower; for, since judgment comes from the activity of him who judges, it is reasonable to believe that he accomplishes this operation entirely by his own means and will, not by any outside constraint as would be the case if we knew things as a consequence of the power and the law of their essence. Now all knowledge enters us through the senses; they are our masters,

> The shortest route by which belief may penetrate
> The human heart and inner chambers of the mind.
> [Lucretius V, 103]

Knowledge begins with the senses and is contained completely in them. After all, we should know nothing more than a stone if we were unaware that there exist sound, odor, light, taste, bulk, weight, softness, hardness, roughness, color, smoothness, width, depth. There we have the foundation and beginning of all the accumulation of our knowledge. And, according to some, knowledge is nothing but sensation. Whoever can force me to contradict the senses holds me by the throat; he could not make me retreat another step. The senses are the beginning and the end of human knowledge:

> You'll find that knowledge of the truth comes to us first
> Through portals of the senses, and their evidence
> Can never be disproved. What then should be believed
> With greater trust than what our senses say is so?
> [Lucretius IV, 478 and 482]

Attribute the smallest possible rôle to the senses, still it will be necessary to recognize that all we learn reaches us by their road and with their help. Cicero says that Chrysippus, having tried to reduce the importance and the power of the senses, imagined against his own stand contrary arguments and oppositions so vehement that he could not answer them. Thereupon Carneades, who was defending the opposite view, boasted that he could use the very arms and words of Chrysippus to oppose him, and for this reason cried out to him: "O wretched man, your very skill has defeated you!" To my mind there is no absurdity so extreme as to maintain that fire does not heat, that light does not illumine, and that there is no weight or hardness in iron; such information the senses bring to us, and there is no belief or knowledge in man which can be compared with it on the score of certitude.

Other creatures may possess other senses, and thus other knowledge.

The first thought I have concerning the senses is that I doubt that man is endowed with all the senses which exist in nature. I see many animals which live a complete and perfect life, some without sight, some without hearing. Who knows whether in us also there may not be lacking one, two, three, and even several other senses? If we lack some one sense, our reason can certainly not discover the lack. It is the privilege of the senses to mark the extreme limits of our perception; there is nothing outside them which can reveal them to us; indeed, one sense cannot even reveal another to us.

> Will ears be able to rebuke the eyes, or touch
> Correct the errors of our ears? Or can our taste
> In turn dispute with touch, or will the nose or eyes
> Confute its evidence and over it prevail?
> [Lucretius IV, 486]

The senses together constitute the extreme limit of our power of knowing;

> To each apart
> Has been assigned its function, and to each its powers.
> [Lucretius IV, 489]

It is impossible to make a man born blind understand that he does not see, impossible to make him desire sight and regret its absence. Therefore we cannot draw any assurance from the fact that our nature is content and satisfied with the senses we possess, since it is in no wise capable of feeling its infirmity and imperfection if it lacks certain senses. It is impossible to say anything to that blind man, through reasoning, argument, or comparison, which will make any notion of light, color, and sight enter his imagination. There is nothing in his experience which can make the meaning clear. When one sees persons blind from birth express the desire to see, it is not because they understand what they are asking for; they have learned from us that they lack something, that they have something to desire which we possess and which they call good, with its effects and consequences. But nevertheless they do not know what it is, nor do they even come near understanding it.

I have seen a gentleman of good family, blind from birth, at least blind so early that he doesn't know what sight is. He is so far from understanding what he lacks that he uses, and employs as we do, words pertaining to sight, and applies them in a quite individual and personal way. When a child for whom he served as godfather was presented to him, he took him in his arms and said, "Goodness, what a handsome child! How good it is to look upon him! What a gay countenance he has!" He will say, as one of us might, "This rooms looks beautiful; it is clear; the sun is shining beautifully." There is even more. Because hunting, tennis, target practice are our pastimes, and he has heard so, he is deeply interested in them, and devotes himself to them, and believes he has the same share in them as we. He is proud of taking part, and derives pleasure from them, and yet is aware of them only through his sense of hearing. They cry out to him that there is a hare when they are in an open space where he can spur on his horse; and then they tell him that a hare has been caught, and he is as proud of his catch as he hears others say they are. He takes the ball in his left hand and drives it as hard as he can with his racket; with his matchlock, he fires at random, and is satisfied when his servants tell him that he is high, or to the side.

How do we know that the human race is not making a similar blunder for lack of some sense or other, and that as a consequence of this lack most of the appearance of things is hidden from us? How do we know that such may not be the source of the difficulties which we encounter in many works of nature? May it not be that various acts of animals which surpass our understanding are produced through the power of some sense which we lack? And may many of them not have through this means a richer and fuller life than we? We perceive the apple through virtually all our senses. We find in it redness, smoothness, odor, and sweetness; apart from that, it may have other qualities, drying or astringent qualities for example, for which we have no corresponding sense. There are qualities in many things which we call occult, as in the magnet the power of attracting iron; is it not probable that there are in nature faculties of sense adapted to judge and perceive them, and that the lack of such faculties is responsible for our ignorance of the true essence of such things? It is by chance some special sense which reveals to roosters the hour of morning and midnight, and stirs them to crow; which teaches hens, prior to any practice or experience, to fear a hawk, and not a goose, nor a peacock, which are larger birds; which warns chickens of the cat's natural hostility toward them, and yet does not make them distrustful of the dog, and puts them on guard against mewing, a somewhat pleasing cry, and not against barking, a harsh and threatening cry; which permits wasps, ants, and rats to choose always the best cheese and the best pear before tasting it, and which gives to the deer, the elephant, or the serpent knowledge of a certain herb capable of healing them.

There is no sense which does not have a great power and does not channel to us an infinite number of perceptions. If we lacked the perception of sounds, harmony, and the voice, that would bring an unimaginable confusion to all the rest of our knowledge. For, apart from what is linked to the special effect of each sense, how many arguments, consequences, and conclusions do we draw concerning other things from the comparison of one sense with another! Let an intelligent man imagine human nature originally produced without the faculty of sight, and conclude how much ignorance and confusion such a lack would contribute to it, how much darkness and blindness there would be in our soul —one will thus see how important for the knowledge of truth it would be to be deprived of another such sense, or of two, or of three, if they are in us. We have formed a truth through the comparison and concurrence of our five senses; but perhaps the accord of eight or ten senses and their contribution were necessary to perceive the truth with certainty and in its essence.

Degree of knowledge dependent on accuracy of sense impressions.

Philosophical schools which deny that man can attain knowledge do so principally because of the uncertainty and weakness of our senses: for, since all knowledge comes to us by means of their intermediary, if they fail in the report they make to us, if they corrupt or alter what they carry to us from outside, if the light which through them filters into our soul is obscured in reaching us, we no longer have anything we can believe. Out of this extreme difficulty are born all these notions: that each object has in itself everything that we find in it; that it has nothing of what we think we find in it; and the Epicureans' notion that the sun is no larger than our sight judges it—

> Whatever it may be, its form no greater is
> Than it may seem as we perceive it with our eyes;
> [Lucretius V, 577]

that the appearances which represent a body large to one who is close to it, and smaller to one who is distant from it, are both true—

> And yet
> We'll not concede one whit the eyes to be at fault;
> Thus blame not on the eyes this error of the mind;
> [Lucretius IV, 379, 386]

and firmly, that there is no deceit in the senses; that we must submit to their mercy, and seek elsewhere reasons to excuse the difference and contradiction which we find in them; that we must even invent any other falsehood and fiction (they go even that far) rather than accuse the senses. Timagoras swore that by pressing his eye or pushing it to the side he had never seen the light of the candle double, and that that illusion derived from the error of the mind, not of the instrument. Of all absurdities, the most absurd in the eyes of the Epicureans is to disavow the power and effect of the senses.

> And thus whatever's seen at any time is true.
> And if the reason fails to understand the cause
> Why what seemed square when viewed close up, should
>   seem from far
> Round in its form, still it is better that we err
> (Because we've found no valid explanation yet)
> In giving for each shape a reason perhaps false
> Than it would be to let slip from our grasp those things
> Which are most clear, to spurn our fundamental truths,
> And thus to overthrow the bases on which life
> And safety rest. For reason fails in every part,
> And life will perish fast unless we dare to trust

The senses, and avoid the falls from dizzy heights
And all the other similar things which must be shunned.
[Lucretius IV, 500]

This counsel of despair, so unphilosophic, declares
nothing other than that human knowledge can be maintained
only by a reason which is unreasonable, mad, and raving;
but even so it is better that man, in order to maintain his
dignity, use it and any other remedy, however fantastic it
may be, rather than admit his essential stupidity—such a
belittling truth! He cannot escape the fact that the senses are
the sovereign masters of his knowledge; but they are uncertain and subject to error in all circumstances. It's on that
ground that we must fight to the limit, and if we lack fair
means, as we do, we must use stubbornness, rashness, impudence.

In case what the Epicureans say is true, namely that we
have no knowledge if the impressions of the senses are false;
and if what the Stoics say is true also, that sense impressions
are so false that they cannot furnish any knowledge—then
we shall conclude, to the contrary of those two great dogmatic sects, that there is no knowledge.

Power of the senses
over reason.

As for the error and uncertainty of the operation of the
senses, each can furnish for himself as many examples as he
pleases, so commonplace are the mistakes and deceptions
which they offer us. Re-echoed by a valley, the sound of a
trumpet seems to come from in front of us, though it comes
from a league behind.

From far, two mountains rising from the surging sea
Seem merged in one, though wide the strait which lies
   between . . .
And hills and fields near which we sail our ship seem fast
To flee astern . . .
If in midstream our dashing steed should stand stock-still,

A force will seem to carry him sideways and bear
His body forcefully against the rushing current.
                              [Lucretius IV, 389, 397, 421]

If we roll a musket ball under the forefinger, the middle finger being crossed above it, we must force ourselves to admit that there is only one ball, so definitely does the sense of touch tell us that there are two. For it seems at every turn that the senses prevail many times over our reason, and force it to receive impressions which it knows and judges to be false. I do not speak of the sense of touch, whose operations are more immediate, more keen, and more substantial, and which upsets so often, by the effect of the pain which it brings to the body, all those fine Stoic resolves, and forces a man to cry out at the pain in his belly even though he may, with the utmost resoluteness, have established in his mind this dogma that colic, like any other illness and pain, is an indifferent matter, having no power in any way to reduce the sovereign happiness and felicity which, through his virtue, the sage has attained.

There is no heart so dull that the sound of our drums and trumpets does not stir it, nor so hard that the sweetness of music does not arouse and titillate it, nor is there a soul so cold that it feels no reverence on observing the somber vastness of our churches, the diversity of ornaments and the order of our ceremonies, and on hearing the worshipful sound of the organ, and the stately and religious harmony of our voices. Even those who enter churches with scorn, feel some thrill in the heart, and a certain awe, which make them question their opinion.

In my own case, I do not consider myself sufficiently self-possessed to listen unmoved to verses of Horace and Catullus sung with a competent voice by a beautiful young mouth.

And Zeno was right to declare that the voice was the flower of beauty. People have sought to convince me that a man whom all we French know had tricked me by reciting

verses he had composed which were not on paper as they
sounded when he recited them, and they assured me that
my eyes would judge them quite otherwise than my ears did,
such power does diction have to give form and worth to
works which depend on it. On that score, Philoxemus was
not unreasonable when, hearing someone interpret badly a
composition of his, he began to break brick which belonged
to that man, saying: "I am destroying what is yours, as you
are ruining what is mine."

How does it happen that those very people who, with a
certain firmness of resolve, have had death inflicted upon
themselves, turned away their face so as not to see the blow
which they had ordered to be dealt? And that those who, for
the sake of their health, wish and order an incision and
cauterization cannot stand the sight of the surgeon's prepa-
rations, his instruments, and his operation? It is clear that
the sense of sight is to have no part in that pain. Are those
not fitting examples to verify the influence that the senses
have over the reason? It matters not that we know these
tresses are borrowed from a page or a lackey, that this blush
came from Spain, and this pale and smooth skin from the
Ocean Sea, still appearance forces us to judge the object
more pleasant and agreeable, against all reason. For in such
things there is nothing of one's own:

> By adornment we are fooled, for gold and gems
> Hide damning flaws: the least part is the maid.
> Behind so many things you seek in vain
> Where what you love may be; this dazzling shield
> Is Cupid's rich device to fool our eyes.
>   [Ovid, *Remedia amoris* I, 343]

How much power those poets attribute to the senses who
make Narcissus madly in love with his own reflection!

> He marvels at those charms for which he is admired;
> Unknowing, he desires himself; and when in praise
> He speaks, he is the object of his own sweet praise;

> He is the seeker and the sought, and equally
> The burning fire, and the loved one for whom he burns.
>   [Ovid, *Metamorphoses* III, 424]

They do the same in making Pygmalion's reason so disturbed by the impression of the sight of his ivory statue that he loves it and treats it as if it were alive!

> He kisses her, and thinks she kisses too,
> And he pursues and throws his arms about her,
> Beneath his fingers feels the yielding flesh,
> And fears lest bruises leave their livid mark
> On tender limbs he has too tightly pressed.
>   [Ovid, *Metamorphoses* X, 256]

Place a philosopher in a cage loosely woven of fine iron wires suspended from the top of the towers of Notre-Dame in Paris. He will recognize by his reason that it is obviously impossible for him to fall from there, and yet (unless he has practiced the roofer's trade) he cannot prevent the sight of that extreme height from terrifying and chilling him. For it is hard enough for us to feel safe along the galleries which are a part of our bell-towers if they are enclosed by an open balustrade, even though they are of stone. There are some who cannot even bear to think of it. Throw a beam across between these two towers of sufficient size that we can walk across it—there is no philosophic wisdom which can give us the courage to walk upon it as we should do if it were on the ground. I have often experienced that in our mountains hereabouts (and yet I am one of those who are only moderately frightened by such things), for I could not endure the sight of that infinite depth without horror nor without a trembling of my calfs and thighs, though I was at least as far from the edge as the length of my own body, and could not have fallen unless I deliberately courted danger. I noticed, too, no matter how great the height might be, so long as on that slope a tree or out-cropping of rock offered itself to reassure our sense of sight and provide something else for it to see, that it furnishes relief and gives assurance, as if it were something from which, in case of a fall, we could receive help. On the other hand, we cannot even look over abrupt and unbroken precipices without dizziness: "so that one cannot look down without the eyes and mind being seized by dizziness." [Livy XLIV, 6] That is an obvious trick played upon us by our eyes. A certain fine philosopher put out his eyes in order to free his mind from the distractions they brought him, and to be able to philosophize in greater liberty.

But, for the same reason, he should also have stopped his ears, which Theophrastus says are the most dangerous instruments we have for receiving violent impressions which disturb and alter us, and he should have deprived himself of all other senses, that is to say of his being and his life. Indeed, they all have that power of governing our reason and our soul. "Also it happens often through the sight of a certain object, often through the deep tone of voices and through songs, that spirits are more violently moved; often, too, through anxiety and fear." [Cicero, De divinatione I, 37] Doctors believe that certain temperaments are disturbed to the point of madness by certain sounds and instruments. I have seen people who couldn't endure without losing patience the sound of a bone being gnawed beneath their table, and there is scarcely a man who is not disturbed at that harsh and penetrating sound that files make rasping iron, and many are moved to anger and hatred by hearing someone chewing near them, or hearing someone whose throat or nasal passages are blocked. Of what use was that ceremonial flute-player of Gracchus, who softened, strengthened, and directed the voice of his master when he spoke publicly in Rome, unless the movement and quality of the sound had the power to disturb and alter the judgment of the listeners? Really there is good cause to celebrate the firmness of that fine instrument, the reason, that lets itself be swung about and changed by the action and effects of so slight a movement of air!

States of mind alter
sense perceptions.

That same deception which the senses bring to our understanding, they receive it in their turn. Our mind sometimes takes revenge in the same way; mind and senses vie with one another in mutual falsehood and deceit. What we see and hear when disturbed by anger, we do not hear as it really is,

> And twin suns and a double Thebes are seen.
> [Virgil, *Aeneid* IV, 470]

The object that we love seems to us more beautiful than it is,

> And thus are to be seen women of all degrees
> Of deformed ugliness among the most beloved
> And thriving in the midst of loftiest respect,
> [Lucretius IV, 1152]

and the one for which we feel antipathy, more ugly than it is. To a man in sorrow and affliction, the light of day seems darkened and gloomy. Our senses are not merely altered, but often completely stupefied by the passions of the soul. How many things do we see that we fail to notice if attention wanders elsewhere?

> Indeed, with things most plainly visible, we know
> That if we fix not on them our attentive gaze
> It is as though they lived far off or long ago.
> [Lucretius IV, 809]

It seems that the soul withdraws within itself and tricks the power of the senses. Thus, both from within and without, man is a prey to weakness and deception.

Those who have compared our life to a dream were right, perhaps more than they thought. When we dream, our soul lives, acts, exercises all its faculties, no more nor less than when it is awake. If it does so less vigorously and somewhat obscurely, the difference is surely not like that between night and full daylight; it is rather like the difference between night and shadow. In the one case it sleeps, and in the other it dozes, more or less. It is always darkness, and even Cimmerian darkness.

We are awake in sleep, and sleep while awake. I do not see so clearly in sleep but, as for my waking life, I never find it sufficiently clear and cloudless. Indeed, sleep in its profundity sometimes puts even dreams to sleep. But our waking is never so complete that it drives away and dissipates completely our reveries, which are the dreams of those awake, and worse than dreams.

Since our reason and our soul receives the fancies and ideas which come to it during sleep, and authorizes the actions of our dreams with the same approval it extends to those of waking hours, why, then, do we not doubt whether our thought, our actions, may not be another dream, and our waking some sort of sleep?

*Relativity of sense
perceptions.*

If the senses are our first judges, it is not merely our own which we must consult, for so far as sense perception is concerned, the animals have as much right as we, if not more. It is certain that some have hearing more keen than man, others keener sight, others a keener sense of smell, or touch, or taste. Democritus said that the gods and the beasts had sensitive faculties far superior to those of man. Now, between the effects of their senses and ours the difference is extreme. Our saliva cleans and dries up our wounds; it kills the serpent.

> In things like these exist such varied differences
> That what is food for some, for others poison is;
> If on a snake a man has spit, it wastes away,
> And oft with its envenomed bite it takes its life.
> [Lucretius IV, 636]

What quality shall we attribute to saliva? Shall we judge it from our viewpoint or from the serpent's? By which of the two senses shall we verify its true essence which we are seeking? Pliny says that there are in India certain "sea hares" which are poison to us, and we to them, so that by a mere touch we kill them: which is really poison, man or the fish? Whom shall we believe—the fish in its judgment on man, or man in his judgment on the fish? A certain quality in the air is harmful to man and not to the ox; a certain other makes the ox fall ill and is harmless to man: which of the two will be, in truth and in essence, a pestilential quality? Those who have jaundice see all things yellowish and more pale than we:

> Thenceforth turn yellow whatsoever things
> A jaundiced man beholds.
>   [Lucretius IV, 332]

Those who have that disease which doctors call "hyposphragma," which is a suffusion of blood under the conjunctiva, see all things red and bloody. These humors which thus change the operations of our sight, how do we know that they may not prevail in beasts and be usual for them? For we see some which have yellow eyes as do people sick with jaundice, others which have bloodshot eyes. It is probable that to them the color of objects seems different from what we see: which judgment of the two is the right one? For it is not said that the essence of things is only in their relation to man. Hardness, whiteness, depth, and bitterness concern the life and experience of animals as they do ours; nature has given to them, as to us, the use of them. When we press the eye, we see the objects we look at stretched in length. Numerous animals have eyes of such a form—that length is then, perhaps, the true shape of that object rather than the one our eyes attribute to it in their usual state. If we press the eye from beneath, things seem double to us,

> Now twofold seem to blaze the flowering flames of lamps,
> Twofold appear men's faces and their bodies too,
>   [Lucretius IV, 450]

if something blocks our ears, or the passage of the ear is narrowed, we receive sounds otherwise than we usually do. Animals which have hairy ears, or which have only a tiny passage instead of an ear, consequently do not hear what we hear, and receive the sound differently. We see at festivals and in theaters that by placing in front of the light of the torches a glass tinted with some color or other, everything which is in that place is made to appear green, or yellow, or purple;

> The hanging awnings, yellow, red, and brown,
> Which in vast theaters, stretched from masts and beams,
> Flutter above, have often this effect.
> They lend their color to the audience;
> The whole appearance of the stage—of men,
> Of women, and of gods—they modify,
> Transmitting as they ripple their own hues.
>   [Lucretius IV, 75]

It is probable that the eyes of the animals, which we see of various colors, make objects appear to them with the colors lent them by their eyes.

To judge the action of the senses, we should first of all have to agree with the beasts, and secondly among ourselves. This accord is singularly lacking. We constantly are involved in disputes because one persons hears, sees, or tastes something in a different way from another, and we debate, as much as about anything else, about the diversity of the impressions which the senses bring us. By the general rule of nature, a child hears, and sees, and tastes, otherwise than a man of thirty, and the latter otherwise than a man of sixty. The senses are for some more obscure and dark; for others, more responsive and keener. We receive things differently according to what we are and how things seem to us. Now how things seem to us is so uncertain and so subject to controversy that it is no longer a miracle if we are told that we may confess that snow seems to us white, but as for establishing whether its essence is in truth such, we could not answer for it. Once this foundation is shaken in this way, all the knowledge in the world necessarily goes off, carried away by the current.

What of the fact that our senses even hinder one another? A painting seems to the eye to have relief, but to the touch it seems flat; shall we say that musk is pleasant or not, when it delights our smell and offends our taste? There are unguents which are good for one part of the body, and which hurt another. Honey is pleasant to the taste, and displeasing to the eye. Those rings that are carved in the form of plumes and that in heraldry they call "endless feathers," there is no eye which can discern their width and which can protect itself against the illusion that in one direction they continue to widen out and in the other to narrow to a point, even when you roll them around your finger; and yet when you handle them they seem to the touch even in width and in all parts alike. . . .

Is it our senses which lend to things these various conditions, while the things themselves have, however, only one? We see this in the bread we eat. It is only bread, but our use makes of it bones, blood, flesh, hair, and nails.

> As food, distributed through body's many parts,
> Out of itself, destroyed, forms other substances.
> [Lucretius III, 703]

The food that the root of the tree sucks up becomes trunk, leaf, and fruit; and though the air remains the same, it becomes, through the intermediary of a trumpet, diversified in a thousand sorts of sounds. Is it, I repeat, our senses which similarly contribute to these objects various qualities, or are they such? And with this doubt as a starting point, how can we resolve their true essence? Moreover, since the accidents of illness, reveries, or sleep make things appear to us other than they appear to the healthy, to the attentive, and to those who are wide awake, is it not likely that our

what is the argument
unreliability of my senses
knowledge
THE UNRELIABILITY OF THE SENSES   117

normal health and our natural humors are capable of giving a being to things in relation to their own condition, and of accommodating them to themselves, as do disordered humors; and that our good health is also capable of furnishing them its particular appearance as disease does? Why should the temperate man not perceive objects in some form peculiarly relative to himself, as the intemperate man does, and why will he not imprint likewise his character upon them?

The surfeited man imputes insipidity to wine; the healthy man flavor; the thirsty man, cool delight.

*Sense impressions can tell us nothing
about things as they are.*

Now since our state accommodates things to itself and transforms them according to itself, we do not know what things are in truth, for nothing comes to us except falsified and altered by our senses. Where the compass, square, and rule are faulty, all the proportions which are drawn from them, all the buildings constructed by their measure, are also necessarily inadequate and deficient. The uncertainty of our senses renders uncertain everything they produce:

> In building if, first off, the rule is not quite true,
> Or if the angle of a square is slightly wrong,
> Or if the level isn't fully accurate,
> Then all things must be out of plumb, askew,
> Twisted and leaning, and the whole so badly ordered
> That it seems doomed to crumble, as straightway it does,
> Betrayed by those defects. So too your reasoning
> On things must needs be warped if it, or anything,
> Is based on errors of the senses.
>
> [Lucretius IV, 513]

Moreover, who will be in a position to judge these differences? Just as we say in religious disputes that we must have a judge not allied to either sect, free from prejudice and attachment (which is not possible among Christians), so the same rule applies here. For if he is old, he cannot judge the feeling of the old, being himself a party to the dispute; so, too, if he is young, healthy, sick, asleep, or awake. We should need someone free of all these qualities so that, without prejudice, he might judge these propositions as indifferent to himself—in other words, we should need a judge who cannot exist.

To judge the impressions which we receive from things, we should need a judicatory instrument; to verify that instrument, we need demonstration; to verify the demonstration, we need an instrument. There is no way out of this dilemma. Since the senses cannot decide our dispute, being full of uncertainty themselves, it must be reasoning. But no reasoning can be established without a prior reasoning, and here we are proceeding backwards without any possible stopping place. Our impressions are not the product of exterior things, but they are conceived through the intermediary of the senses; and the senses do not understand the exterior object, but only their own feelings; and thus the impression and appearance are not derived from the object, but only from the feeling and sensation of the senses, and that feeling and the object are entirely different things. Therefore he who judges by appearances, judges by something other than the object. As for saying that the feelings of the senses bring to our spirit the quality of exterior objects by resemblance, how can the spirit and the understanding be sure of that resemblance, having by themselves no contact with exterior things? We have a parallel situation when one who doesn't know Socrates sees his portrait, and cannot tell whether it resembles him. Now if one wished just the same to judge by appearances, it could not be by all appearances, for they are in conflict with one another through their contradictions and discrepancies, as experience shows us. Shall some selected appearances govern the rest? It will be necessary to verify the selected appearance by another, the second by a third, and thus it will never be complete.

The constant flux of things
keeps us from grasping
their essence.

Finally, there is no constant existence, either of our own being or of that of objects. We ourselves, and our judgment, and all mortal things, flow and are carried away unceasingly. Thus nothing certain can be established relative to one thing and the other, the judge and the thing judged being in continual change and movement.

We have no contact with being because every human nature is always moving between birth and death, giving of itself only an obscure appearance and shadow, and an uncertain and feeble impression. And if, by chance, you are determined to capture its essence, it will be neither more nor less than trying to seize running water, for the more you grasp and press what by its nature flows in all directions, the more you will lose what you have sought to hold firm in your hands. Thus, all things being subject to passing from one change to another, the reason, seeking, a true essence in them, is deceived, not being able to seize anything subsistent and permanent because everything is either coming into being and is not yet at all, or is beginning to die before it is born. Plato used to say that bodies never had any existence, but that they had certainly a birth. He believed that Homer had made Oceanus father of gods, and Thetis their mother, in order to show us that all things are in perpetual flux, change, and variation—an opinion common to all philosophers before his time, as he says, with the single exception of Parmenides, who denied that things had movement, while Plato considered the power of movement of great importance. Pythagoras said that all matter is flowing and gliding; the Stoics that there is no present time, and that what we call the present is only the point of contact between the future and the past; Heraclitus said that never can a man step twice into the same river; Epicharmus that he who borrowed money in the past does not owe it now, and he who last night was invited to come this morning to lunch, comes today uninvited since they are no longer the same people—they have become others; and Epicharmus further declares that there could not be a mortal substance twice in the same state for, by its rapid propensity to change, sometimes it is dispersed, sometimes brought together; it comes, and then goes away. So that what begins to be born never reaches a state of perfection of being, inasmuch as that birth is never complete and never stops, as being at an end, but, from the seed, continues always to change and evolve from one thing into another. Similarly, the human seed becomes first in the mother's womb a formless fruit, then an infant with form, then, having left the womb, a nursling; afterwards he becomes a boy, then in due course a stripling, later a grown man, then a man of mature years, and finally a decrepit old man. So the subsequent age and generation always destroys and spoils the preceding one:

> Years change the nature of the whole wide world;
> Out of one state, another must emerge,
> And nothing may remain in its old form.
> All things move on; nature transforms them all;
> None may resist her law compelling change.
>
> [Lucretius V, 828]

And then we stupidly fear one sort of death when we have already passed through, and continue to pass through, so many others. For not only, as Heraclitus said, is the death of fire a generation of air, and the death of air a generation of water, but more obviously can we observe it in ourselves. The flower of age dies and passes when old age steals upon us, and youth ends in the blossoming of maturity, and childhood in youth, and infancy in childhood, and yesterday dies in today, and today has its death in tomorrow; and there is nothing which remains nor which is always the same. For if indeed we do remain always the same, how does it happen that we now enjoy one thing, and now another? How is it that we like contrary things or hate them, that we praise them or blame them? How do we have different feelings, not retaining any longer the same feeling toward the same thing? For it is not reasonable that without change we should acquire other feelings, and what undergoes change does not remain the same, and if it is not the same, it does not exist either. But when the being of a thing is changed, its essence is no longer the same, and it becomes always something different. And consequently the senses are deceitful and lie by their very nature, taking what appears for what really is, for lack of knowing clearly what being is.

Nothing exists, eternally unchanged, except God. But what then really does exist? Only that which is eternal, that is to say, that which has never had any birth and will never have any end, and to which time never brings any change. For time is a fleeting thing, which appears like a shadow, with matter always flowing and passing, without ever remaining stable and permanent. To it belong these words: *before* and *after,* and *has been* or *will be,* which straightway show beyond question that it is not anything which *is.* For it would be a great stupidity and error to declare that that *is* which has not yet attained being, or which has already ceased to be. And as for those words: *present, instant, now,* by which it seems that principally we form and support the notion of time, in the very discovery of it reason destroys time swiftly and utterly, for it cleaves it at once and divides it into future and past, as wishing to see it necessarily divided in two.

So it is with the nature which is measured as with the time which measures it. For there is nothing in it which either remains or is subsistent, but all things in it are born, or being born, or dying. For this reason it would be a sin to say of God, who is the only being who *is,* that he was or will be. For those terms are indicative of the decline, passing, or accidents of what cannot endure nor remain in being. Therefore one must conclude that God alone *is,* not according to some measure of time, but according to an immutable and fixed eternity, not measured by time, nor subject to any decline; before which nothing is, nor will be afterwards, neither anything newer nor more recent, but a being really existent which by a single *now* fills the forever; and there is nothing which really is except him—without our being able to say "He has been," or "He will be"—without beginning and without end.

*Only by God's grace can man rise above
the common status of mankind.*

To this most religious conclusion of a pagan,[10] I wish to add only this remark of a witness[11] of similar condition to bring to a close this long and boresome discourse, which would furnish me material to go on for ever. "What a vile and abject thing man is," he says, "if he does not rise above humanity." That's a clever remark and a useful desire, but it is nonetheless absurd. For to make the handful bigger than the hand, the armful greater than the arm, and to hope to make a stride longer than the stretch of our legs, that is impossible and against nature. Nor can man rise above himself and above humanity, for he can see only with his eyes and seize only with his hands. He will rise if God by special grace holds out to him his hand; he will rise, abandoning and renouncing his own means, and letting himself be raised and lifted up by purely divine means.

It is up to our Christian faith, not Seneca's Stoic virtue, to seek that divine and miraculous metamorphosis.

---

[10] The preceding development is borrowed in large part from Plutarch.

[11] Seneca, in the preface to Book I of *Quaestiones naturales*.